The Recruiting Process
A Baseball Recruiting Guidebook
for High School Players
and Their Families

WALTER BEEDE
&
BUTCH BACCALA

Beede Baseball Publishing LLC
Lynn MA 01902

https://www.baseballprocess.com
https://www.themastersofbaseball.com

DEDICATIONS

I would like to dedicate this book to my brother Frederick D. Beede, November 10, 1968 – June 19, 2022. He was my hero in every sense of the word. I miss him terribly. I never saw a rock that he couldn't jump off or ride over. FDB. FHB. KFB. TJB. BDB. BDB.

RIDE ON BROTHER.

—Walter Beede

I've watched a great deal of baseball over the years with my baseball friends, often away from my family members. I've held close to my heart what I felt should be a road map and a way of baseball growth that would eventually define a path of success. Here between these covers is that road map. It's a direction that has been lived by both Walter and me.

Whether it has been Walter's journey as both a college coach and parent of an incredibly special player, or my journey as a twenty-five-year MLB scout, together Walter and I have over 70 years of baseball experience at its highest levels. For both of us, baseball is life. We hope you learn from our baseball lives, and that the experiences from our own baseball journeys help your family navigate your journey.

Let your son, your family enjoy the process and not feel the need to race through it. Use the information in this book to define your path to success not only in baseball, but to construct a plan for a winning life.

Simply put, this book is for you, the athletes and families. It is our hope that the game brings you the happiness it has brought us: a legacy of love for a sport that has now defined as our lives. We wish you the absolute best with your journey within the game. Enjoy the journey and we hope to help with your destination!

—Butch Baccala

CONTENTS

FOREWORD

by Tyler J. Beede

As I am writing this foreword, I am reminded of the days when my brother and I would play all kinds of games in the backyard or playground. We always created scenarios such as "bases loaded, two outs, Tyler Beede on the mound trying to close this one out." Whatever the season was, we were playing a sport. I played football from six years old through my high school senior year. I never once heard my father say anything about getting hurt or asking me to focus on any one sport. His stock answer was, "It is your life; if you love it, play it." Auburn, Massachusetts is a small town in the central part of the state. My earliest memories of being an athlete were that my father was always the one taking me to practices and games. I played hockey, soccer, basketball, football, and baseball, and ran track. And the one question my father would always ask both my brother and me was "Are you having fun?"

My brother and I would always attend my father's practices when he was a head coach at the high school and college levels. He allowed us to join in with team workouts, but only if we were prepared to do the drills exactly how his players were doing them. He always taught us that whenever we went between the lines we needed to be mentally and physically prepared to take part and compete. As a college head coach, my dad would often take us on recruiting trips to watch high school–age athletes play.

Whenever he liked a potential recruit, he would circle the player number and write "keeper" next to his name. I remember their names as if it were yesterday—Mike "Carbs," Cory "Shep," Joey "Bling," Matt "Tittle," Dan Ortiz, and my childhood idols, Keith and Kevin Renaud. I remember being with my dad while he was watching them play and thinking, "These guys are unreal!" How was he going to convince these students to play for Becker College?

It is important to note that my father took over a new NCAA Division 3 program that was *0-101* its first few years of Division 3–level play. During my dad's time there, the college moved from junior college to NCAA; during that transition the program struggled to get serious, college-caliber talent. It took creativity to get the program going. My father accepted the position and donated his salary back to the program so they could go on a southern trip to start the season. A southern trip for a northeast school was an absolute must to recruit higher caliber student-athletes.

As I watched my father interact with student-athletes and their families, I was always amazed at how prepared he was for each individual recruit. For instance, there was a shortstop from Portland Maine. He was good. Somehow my father was able to convince him that his future at the college level and beyond was at second base. On the ride home, I asked him "why would you move that player from shortstop to second base?" He said, "foot speed is critical at shortstop and his time to first base was 4.5 and 4.7, so he would not have required foot speed to play shortstop." I remember that ride home thinking that my father saw the smallest details of all the students he went to see. His process of recruiting was to see the best student-athletes and provide them with a detailed game plan that would help them have a quality college experience.

His diligence is what he would term a separator. This is what makes my father unique. He sees the college experience as something that he missed out on. He wants to make sure student-athletes understand that the college recruiting process is a forty-year plan. I remember the day my father had to choose between his love of coaching and watching his sons play baseball. I called him during his conference championships to let him know that I had just hit my first homerun over a fence. The silence on the other end of the phone was a long one. I knew that he really was upset that his coaching career was going to limit his ability to watch my brother and me play.

The next month my father stepped away from coaching and began to collaborate with us as well as local student-athletes about our playing experiences. My brother and I did not play travel baseball of any kind until we were fourteen. I remember playing with my friends at the Babe Ruth and American Legion levels. In fact, I played American Legion baseball at thirteen at the recommendation of former Boston Red Sox catcher Rich Gedman. My father simply let us enjoy our local community and friends until we got to the high school level. My brother and I always practiced with my father's college athletes and learned the game by watching and taking part with older players. I feel that these opportunities to watch older players at the high school and college levels allowed me to understand what I was preparing for.

Once I entered the eighth grade, my father began to make a series of decisions that would alter my future as a college athlete. Before attending any showcases or college camps my father suggested that I play on a summer team that featured advanced players so that I could truly measure my abilities. As a fifteen-year-old, I played on a 16u Team. The Canes National team consisted of several athletes who'd verbally committed to programs such as Florida University, Miami University, University of South Carolina, and North Carolina University. During that summer, I saw the caliber of student-athlete that I needed to prepare to compete with and against.

After that summer, I immersed myself in a strength program at Cressey Performance. Then my father and I began what I would term my college recruiting process. My father always was one step, if not two steps, ahead during my college recruiting process. I knew he was drawing experience from his own career as a talented high school player who bypassed college to sign with the Chicago Cubs, but he took the route of educator, encourager, and father when he could have successfully taken the role of coach and enforcer. He educated me on each process, each decision, and each opportunity I had in front of me. He encouraged me to think on it, weigh the pros and cons, trust my gut, and move forward with each decision. As a father he believed in me and instilled confidence in me at each turn. Whether it was the decision to choose Vanderbilt over schools such as UVA, LSU, UNC and USC, or the choice to turn down a life changing opportunity to play for the Blue Jays after the 2011 MLB draft, I always felt I was prepared for each of those massive decisions and given the personal time to choose for myself. I was also fully supported no matter which choice I would eventually make.

Pops has always been one step ahead of the college, and MLB draft, process. He does his homework. He is well connected, and he is trusted as a valuable resource by college coaches around the country. He has committed his life to this great game and helping families work through these incredibly challenging and overwhelming decisions. He does not do it for the praise or recognition; he does it so that some aspiring baseball student-athlete, with the same dreams that I had, can experience the same joy and accomplishment as I have been blessed to experience because of the help of my father.

The three books that my father has written, *Fun over Fear*, *The Process*, and *The Recruiting Process*, were written from my father's heart. They simply speak for his love of the game. These books are filled with his stories, opinions, and, most of all, feelings that will help families find their way on their own journeys. I have heard stories from hundreds of families over the years about how my father helped a student-athlete have a quality experience at the college level. Many of the original student-athletes he coached now have young children of their own, and they reach out to my father with questions. Thank you for finding your way to this book. I hope it offers you valuable insight into your son's college recruiting process. I know one thing about my father: if you have a question, he will help you find the answer.

In closing let me share this final story. On August 15, 2011, I was faced with the biggest decision of my life. There was a midnight deadline that night by which I had to choose between attending Vanderbilt University or becoming a member of the Toronto Blue Jays. At my home that evening were family members, as well as my advisor at the time. For two months I had gone back and forth with all the pros and cons that both decisions presented. Many of my friends had already signed their contracts or had started summer classes at their university of choice.

At 11:45 p.m., I asked my father to step outside with me. I looked my father right in the eyes and asked, "What do you think I should do?" As he collected his thoughts, I expected him to join the rest of the group and suggest that I take the life altering money being offered. Instead he asked me a question. "What if you are good as they think you are and you attend Vanderbilt, and you help that program win its first ever national championship? What if you attend Vanderbilt as an eighteen to twenty-two-year-old and meet lifelong friends or meet your future wife? It is easy for adults to tell you that you can go to college at any time in your life and that pro baseball is a once in a lifetime opportunity. My point is that you can only be a part of a college experience at this stage of your life. If you are as good as people think you are, there will be another opportunity. Believe in yourself and in your plan."

That year Vanderbilt University won its very first men's national championship in any sport, becoming 2014 CWS National Champions. And I met my future wife during the College World Series. Three years later, I was drafted seven slots higher by the San Francisco Giants as the fourteenth overall pick in the MLB Draft.

I am beginning to think Big Walt might have himself a crystal ball!

Tyler J. Beede
Vanderbilt University, 2017
Current Pittsburg Pirate
Former San Francisco Giant

THE ROAD AHEAD

I am writing this supplement to The Process to help high school students and their families make wise choices as they consider all their options as they transition from life at home in high school, to life out in the world as an adult.

For most readers, I am strongly of the opinion that your best path forward is to use your baseball-playing ability for the absolute best education you can receive for the career you wish to pursue after your playing days are over. Since all decisions have trade-offs, make a wise decision with forty-year benefits!

In the summer of 1981, weeks after I graduated high school, the Chicago Cubs selected me in the thirteenth round of the MLB Draft, and I chose a career in professional baseball over a scholarship offer to play at Arizona State. After my playing days were over, I coached all levels from youth to high school to American Legion to NCAA. My two sons played college baseball—one at a major Southeastern Conference school (Vanderbilt) and the other in the JUCO/NAIA ranks (LSU-Eunice and LSU-Alexandria). After his playing days, Kyle started his adult career in coaching. The San Francisco Giants drafted Tyler, and he currently pitches for the Pittsburgh Pirates.

In over forty years of post–high school baseball, I've seen it all. I'm putting it together here for you so you and your family might avoid some of the pitfalls that we've faced as a family and seen other families face. My goal is to help each of you make the wisest decision possible with the best long-term benefit, given the wide range of options on your plate.

The most important thing for each of you is to be honest with yourself about your ability to play, your desire to play, and the impact each college you are considering might have on your post-playing career options.

If you are a youth baseball player or parents of a student-athlete looking to continue playing baseball after high school, I understand the path ahead. The purpose of this supplement to The Process is to help you understand each of the seven options available to you:

- NCAA (National Collegiate Athletic Association) Division 1
- NCAA Division 2
- NCAA Division 3
- NAIA (National Association of Intercollegiate Athletics)
- JUCO (Junior College)
- Post-Graduate School
- Hanging up the spikes

I know that whichever path you choose, navigating the process is extremely difficult. I want to provide you with as much information as possible so you can make a wise decision.

As we move forward, I will explain the different sets of recruiting rules for each NCAA division, NAIA, and JUCO, introductory-level information for post-graduate schools, and things to consider prior to deciding if you have played your final competitive, organized baseball game. Each choice comes with different recruitment rules, calendars, expectations and, of course, levels of play. The goal is to be informed so you can be prepared to play in whichever division you feel is *your* best fit.

THE OPTIONS

This chapter's goal is to break down what a student-athlete can expect to see and experience at each level of competition after high school. My sole goal is to help recruits and their families make the most informed decision possible about what is the best fit for them. Recruits should use this information to create their target school list. I always recommend they include a mix of schools at all levels.

Parents, remember that this is *their* choice. When a student-athlete puts more into and takes ownership of the decision process, the odds go way up that it will be the best decision for them. They are the ones who must live with the choices they make. This decision is one of the biggest they will ever make, and one of the hardest. The likelihood that your child will find his career, spouse, and forever friends is extremely high that it will be where he goes to college. The more options recruits start with, the more chances you will have to find a school that matches you athletically, academically, and socially. Hopefully, this supplement, the questionnaire found later in "The Decision Process," and the rest of the information included will help our student-athletes focus their lists and simplify the decision-making process.

As you the parent—and hopefully your child—read the book, please keep in mind that this is an open-ended, ongoing discussion that should be seen through your child's eyes. Remember that it truly is about what *they* want and need. This is not to say that a parent should not have input, especially when it comes to the financial limitations and needs of the family.

In that regard, the three most important numbers in college baseball are 11.7, 35 and 27. The first number is the number of scholarships available to *almost* every Division 1 program in the country. The second number is the number of players carried at the varsity level of Division 1 programs. The third number is the number of players on a Division 1 roster who are eligible to receive a *partial* scholarship.

Every school decides differently how to divide these 11.7 scholarships among their players on their rosters. Due to different budget constraints in athletic departments across the country, not every school is receiving sufficient funding to supply all 11.7 scholarships. And so, the coaching staff has fewer scholarship dollars to award to prospective recruits. The reality is there are *very* few full scholarships in college baseball. It is extremely important to understand that up front.

Now, let's look at the levels of competition in college baseball.

The Levels of Competition

There are just under 1,700 college baseball programs in the United States, and five major governing bodies that oversee them:

- NCAA Division 1
- NCAA Division 2
- NCAA Division 3
- NAIA
- NJCAA

Each level offers its own unique experiences, opportunity for development and growth, and culture, with varying degrees of skill and competitiveness required of student-athletes. All of them should be in play when deciding where your best fit is, because athletes at every level can find a way to reach the major league. Once at any college, if someone can play then professional scouts will find them. Several elite MLB players have come out of the smaller levels, so do not let that be a deterrent if that smaller school is your best fit. The key is to get into a college program where you can get on the field.

NCAA

I strongly suggest registering your athlete at the NCAA's Eligibility Center (https://web3.ncaa.org/ecwr3/). The NCAA uses that to make sure students meet its academic and amateur athlete requirements.

Within the NCAA there are three divisions. While there are material differences within schools at each level, there are a few general tendencies to compare one level to another, as follows:

School Characteristics	Division 1	Division 2	Division 3
Player Skill Level	Highest	High	—
% of MLB Draft Picks	Highest	High	Smaller
Strength of Facilities & Player Support Tools	Highest	—	—
Athletic Department Budget Size	Largest	Varies	Varies
Variety of Majors & Graduate School	Greatest	—	High
Academic Emphasis	—	—	Highest
Time Requirements	Highest	High	—
School Size	Varied	Smaller	Smallest
Roster Size	35	39	34
Players Receiving Scholarship Money	27	Varies	0
Minimum % Scholarship Awarded	25%	N/A	N/A
Non-Academic Grants Awarded	Varies	Varies	Highest

NCAA Division 1: The Highest Level of College Baseball

Overall, Division 1 programs have larger roster sizes and higher turnover compared to other levels of play. Playing time is at a premium. Division 1 schools usually have broader undergraduate curriculum and graduate school options. Academic grants and several aid packages are available; some are need based. Grade point average (GPA), SAT, or ACT requirements are typically higher.

While NCAA Division 1 is the highest and most well-known division to compete in, it should not be the only level that student-athletes focus on.

Please do not let the name of the school be the only (or even main) thing you use to try to determine your best fit. NCAA Divisions 2 and 3 are extremely competitive academically and athletically, and there are many Division 2 and 3 schools that can compete at the Division 1 level. NAIA and JUCO schools can also provide a bridge to NCAA schools.

PRO TIP: Take charge of your academic eligibility and challenge yourself to do the best you can. The NCAA Division 1 and 2 initial eligibility worksheet is available online. http://fs.ncaa.org/Docs/ eligibility_center/DI_and_DII_Worksheet.pdf

---

NCAA Division 2: Don't Sleep On Them—Find Your Fit!

In Division 2, the time mandated towards baseball is like Division 1. Nine athletic scholarships can be divided amongst thirty-nine athletes. Schools tend to make up for it by being more creative in finding money for athletes: grants, academic money, need-based grants, financial aid, etc. Facilities quality is more varied. Schools are usually smaller in size, but can be stronger academically, while still having above average baseball programs.

Some of the better Division 2 schools have top-notch indoor facilities, which should be part of your research into cold-weather schools. Division 2 also likely offers underclassmen the opportunity to get on the field faster.

NCAA Division 3: Student First

Division 3 is made up of mostly smaller, private liberal arts schools. Among the NCAA divisions, Division 3's rules around participation time create the greatest balance between academics and athletics.

Division 3 schools offer academic scholarships and need-based assistance, but not athletic scholarships. Student-athletes at this level are the guys that honestly love the game the most. They're the dirt ballers, the grinders. Players seek stronger academics with the opportunity to play beyond high school. They tend to be very vocal and enthusiastic about the game, while playing to win.

The quality of the academics you are exposed to way overshadows the limitations of the baseball program. Players play for love of the game—to extend their baseball careers as long as they can. Schools can be found that have top notch facilities as well. Also, Division 3 schools are usually a better value.

NAIA: Smaller Campuses

While there are notable exceptions to this, NAIA schools tend to be less well-known nationally, and occasionally regionally, than NCAA schools. They usually have smaller campus sizes and tend to have lower academic standards than the NCAA schools. They are still four-year universities that offer a great balance between athletics and academics. There are some amazing schools with fantastic academics, campuses, facilities, and playing fields. NAIA programs are aggressive with JUCO transfers looking for four-year programs. NAIA programs have players selected in the MLB draft each year. NAIA does not have roster limitations. In fact, it is not uncommon to see anywhere from 35 to 90+ players. With some programs having full JV teams, the numbers can get quite big.

NJCAA: A Place to Develop

The National Junior College Athletic Association (NJCAA) is the governing body for JUCO schools. Throughout this book, if I'm talking about a specific division I'll say something like NJCAA Division 1; if I'm talking about junior college in general I'll say JUCO.

JUCOs are two-year schools and award associates degrees in a wide variety of areas from accounting to nursing to welding and other trades. These schools have a wide variety of advantages over NCAA or NAIA schools and are great options for many students. Common benefits include lower cost of attendance, time for development as both a student and an athlete, and proximity. The NJCAA operates in three distinct levels of play, just like the NCAA.

It's important to note that at NJCAA level, a student-athlete is eligible for the MLB draft each of their two years. NJCAA Division 1 is looking for potential MLB draft-worthy players or Power 5 NCAA Division 1 players (those who could end up in the ACC, Big Ten, Big 12, Pac-12, or SEC). They also get a lot of student-athletes sent to them from Power 5 programs.

Many baseball players and other athletes decide to spend two years at a JUCO and then transfer to a four-year university, oftentimes with their core academic requirements already out of the way. If you are a high school athlete who needs some more time to improve your academics or athletic skills, going to a JUCO and then transferring to a four-year university is a great possibility. It is also important to stress that most athletes seeking opportunities to play after high school can do so much more affordably at a JUCO than either an NCAA or NAIA school.

Ivies and Academies

The Ivy League (Brown, Columbia, Cornell, Dartmouth, Harvard, Princeton, University of Pennsylvania, and Yale) are in a category all their own because they supply a vastly unique experience when compared to the typical NCAA university. While all eight universities take part in NCAA Division 1 athletics and field baseball teams full of talented players, they do not offer athletic scholarships. The emphasis has always been on academics. I cannot recommend a student to consider these schools unless their academic pursuits are at the top of their mind. I also am not afraid to recommend the Ivy League schools to any athlete with dreams of playing in the MLB. While Ivy League schools do not award athletic scholarships—and while they usually have the highest tuition costs—they also are among the most generous schools in the world with need-based tuition grants. Additionally, many Ivy League schools have club (i.e., non-varsity) teams, which are a fantastic choice and a lot of *fun*. Club teams provide many students with an opportunity to keep playing the game they love.

There are also the Near Ivies and Public Ivies (Cal-Berkeley, Duke, Michigan, North Carolina, Northwestern, Rice, Stanford, Tulane, UCLA, Wake Forest, Vanderbilt, and Virginia). These public and private institutions are very academically demanding, like the Ivy League. However, they take part in other conferences and do award athletic scholarships. This is not intended to be an exhaustive list of universities with high focus on academic qualities. It is important that I include the NCAA Division 3 New England Small College Athletic Conference (NESCAC) on this list. With schools such as Bates, Bowdoin, Amherst, Williams, Wesleyan, Colby, Hamilton, Trinity and Tufts, they offer extremely high-level academic degrees and programs.

For uniquely motivated student-athletes there are the service academies: U.S. Air Force Academy, U.S. Naval Academy, and U.S. Military Academy at

West Point. While not all service academies field baseball teams, all of them require and deserve their own category. They have an extremely specific and rigorous set of requirements academically, athletically, and in service. Post-graduation military service time is mandatory for any cadet who stays for their final two years. It takes a vastly different student-athlete with unique goals to choose this option. It is not for everyone. But it can be the most rewarding of all the options.

The Safety Net

Even if you have a dream of playing in the major leagues one day, I cannot say and stress this enough: do everything you can to trade your athletic ability for academic excellence! Baseball ends for everyone sometime, but an education lasts a lifetime.

Therefore, when you have a student-athlete who may be stronger athletically than in the classroom, you can create what I call a "safety net". A student-athlete can apply and commit to a JUCO, an NAIA, and an NCAA program at the same time because all are different organizations and levels. This creates a safety net that allows student-athletes to make last minute decisions based on transcripts, GPA, and roster spots.

It is also important to note that if you listen to top college baseball coaches at all levels, they will tell you they are slowing the process down. They want to see academic and athletic development throughout high school. They also want to see how student-athletes compete and deal with the ebbs and flow within the game. Coaching staffs are now focused on watching and evaluating during games rather than just seeing a student-athlete at a showcase. We will cover this in detail throughout this supplement to *The Process*.

WHAT COLLEGE RECRUITERS AND SCOUTS ARE LOOKING FOR

In this chapter, we'll try to give student-athletes some guidelines for measuring where they may stand as a ballplayer, and in what level they may truly fit and realistically strive for. I feel that it is important to add the grading scale that is used when evaluating a college student-athlete or possible MLB draft–caliber athlete.

Student-athletes are evaluated on five tools: speed, arm strength, fielding, hitting for average, and hitting for power. Recruiters and scouts look at measurables (like 60-yard run time), game performance, and statistical results to give each tool a grade on a 20–80 scale. Those grades give you the student-athlete's overall future potential (OFP) and a label that goes with it.

- **80—Superior Prospect**. Hall of Fame–type Player. All-Star every year. Best in the game.
- **70—Excellent Prospect**. All-Star performer. One of the best all time at his position. Big tools.
- **60—Good Prospect**. Occasional All-Star. Consistently considered among the ten best at his position. A carrying tool (the tool that separates the player from others at the position) is usually the bat. Power or Hitting Average is above the Normal
- **50—Average Prospect**. Chance to be everyday MLB Player. Will be a player that has a solid tool or skill but doesn't have the ability to be one of your top players. More defensive than offensive. Utility Value. Does just enough to stay in lineup every day.
- **40—Below Average Prospect**. Backup Player. Major League ability but doesn't perform to a level of everyday contributor. Relieve a starter but weaknesses exposed if playing in everyday role. Too many of these players on a team will make for losing record team. Role player.

MLB Overall Future Potential Chart, 20–80 Grading Scale

Grade	Tool is Called	Fastball Velocity	Batting Average	Home Runs	RHH to 1B	LHH to 1B	60 yd Run
80	Excellent	97	.320	40+	4.00	3.90	6.3
75		96	.310	35-40	4.05	3.95	6.4
70	Good	95	.300	30-35	4.10	4.00	6.5
65		94	.290	27-30	4.15	4.05	6.6
60	Plus	93	.280	23-27	4.20	4.10	6.7
55	Strong Average	92	.270	19-22	4.25	4.15	6.8
50	Avg	90-91	.260	15-18	4.30	4.20	6.9-7.0
45	Near Average	89	.250	12-15	4.35	4.25	7.1
40	Below Average	88	.240	8-12	4.40	4.30	7.2
35		87	.230	5-8	4.45	4.35	7.3
30	Marginal	86	.220	3-5	4.50	4.40	7.4

RHH = right-handed hitter   LHH = left-handed hitter
1B = first base   yd = yard

Position by Position Breakdown of Necessary Tools and Playing Ability

I have broken down these positions first by what colleges are looking for. For position players, this is a prioritized list of the five tools; every position has a role to play on the field and in the lineup. Then I get into a much more detailed description of what college coaches and pro scouts will be looking for.

What Do College Baseball Scouts Look for in A Pitcher?

- Velocity is 84 miles per hour (MPH) consistently; up to 95+ MPH
- At least 1 strikeout (K) per inning pitched
- Strong arm; durable
- Mentally tough; knows how to finish hitters
- Able to handle high-pressure situations/good heartbeat
- High dexterity and feel for throwing a baseball
- Good body control for repeatability of mechanics
- Three levers that work in sequence: elbow–wrist–fingers
- Extremely competitive
- Strike throwers of a minimum of two pitches
- Ground ball-inducing secondary pitches

- Competes and gets soft contact
- Keeps team in games

Fastball

The first area of focus when evaluating a pitcher is the ability to command the glove-side fastball. Pitchers who can locate their fastball in/out will always be highly sought after. Fastball command is the foundation of all evaluations by college coaches and MLB scouts. Velocity and movement determine college-level ability. In today's metrics-driven game, high spin rates and vertical and horizontal movement matter.

PRO TIP: Fastball command and control are a must at college and professional levels.

Changeup

Having a good changeup is a true separator when college coaches and MLB scouts are evaluating a potential starting pitcher. Most pitchers that become bullpen arms lack a true feel for a changeup, which is considered a true third pitch. The ability to command a changeup along with the ability to throw the pitch in hitting counts (2-0, 3-1 etc.) can elevate a pitcher's potential college opportunity.

Recruiters and scouts evaluate the movement of the pitch, velocity of pitch (MPH separation from fastball), the deception of release, and delivery.

Breaking Ball

The type of spin and break on a slider or curveball are evaluated.

- Depth and shape of break. Is it 12-6 curveball or more of a cut fastball/slider?
- Is the break late and sharp?
- Is there a hump in the pitch that advanced hitters will be able to lay off?
- Deception of release. How similar is the release of a breaking ball to a player's release of fastball? Is the pitcher able to tunnel the breaking ball on the same plane as the fastball?

Delivery

Delivery is about at balance at foot strike, control of the body, coordination of the body, the ability of the upper and lower body to work together in proper sequence, alignment to the plate, plane of shoulders, amount of effort exerted through motion, consistency of mechanics, and repeatability of mechanics.

Arm Action

There's a lot to arm action: arm stroke (path the arm takes out of the glove), arm path (path of the arm through release), arm speed through release, whether the pitcher is using all three levers (elbow–wrist–fingers), and arm lay down (range of motion). How does the arm complete through release? What's the pitcher's ability to repeat consistently, and the amount of effort exerted through release? Whether the arm is working around a pitcher's core or through a pitcher's center will matter regarding strike zone consistency.

Presence and Mound Demeanor

Scouting pitchers can seem intensive. College coaches and MLB scouts believe pitcher evaluation is easier than other positions because players will showcase their abilities right away. Factors like arm strength, strike zone command, pitch movement, and delivery can all be analyzed from a visual standpoint. Younger pitchers should not get caught up or concerned with a radar gun. Show that you can pitch first, and velocity will follow. Where scouting pitchers becomes more in-depth is evaluating a player's ability to use these physical skills during a game.

Presence is subtler. Scouts are looking for body language, a calm but bulldog approach. What are they saying without words on the mound? Do they say "I got this!" with their steely determination, or is it the dreaded deer in the headlights look?

Desire to Challenge

College coaches and MLB scouts look for pitchers who like to challenge hitters. A pitcher might have the physical *skills* to strike out hitters, but are they *willing* to attack a hitter for a needed strikeout? They're looking for confidence on the mound, confidence in their stuff, and throwing strikes that show there's a plan to challenge a hitter. Read that last one again: throwing strikes that show there's a plan.

They want pitchers who do not fear contact and show an ability to create weak contact on batted balls in play. Does the pitcher make hitters make decisions that allow the game to move fast? This keeps infielders and outfielders on their toes and involved in the flow of the game. Going after hitters and understanding game situations can showcase a strong field presence. The will to challenge hitters, rather than finessing around the zone, can show confidence and mental strength.

Mixing it Up

Aside from mental toughness, it can also be beneficial to look for athletes with multiple pitches. The ability to throw secondary pitches in hitting counts will always be seen as a strong separator by college coaches and scouts. The ability to change the speed of the game and keep hitters on their toes is a premium and desired skill set for pitchers.

Physical attributes

When college coaches and scouts are evaluating pitchers, they will ask high school or travel ball coaches lots of questions. Is the pitcher going to grow more? How tall are his parents? Has he physically matured yet, or does he still have room to fill out? If a high-school player hasn't fully matured yet and is currently throwing 83 mph on a radar gun, it can almost be certain that he'll be adding more velocity as he gets bigger and stronger.

What kind of body type does he have—long and lean, or bulky and compact? Coaches are looking for pitchers that will be able to eat innings. They want a reliable arm that is going to last, a big, durable body and a strong lower half. Pitchers who have lower half size and strength will get noticed right away.

Intangibles

I often get asked what intangibles college coaches and pro scouts are really looking for when it comes to pitchers. One of the first questions they want to see answered is, Is he emotionally mature? Can he handle the pressure of pitching in big games and big situations, or does he let mistakes rattle him? What type of body language does he show in moments of stress? Does he control the running game and game tempo?

Coaches and scouts are looking for guys who want the ball. Coaches and scouts aren't just watching for actions during a game. They usually watch a player from the moment they reach the field. What does the pitcher's pregame routine look like? How does he interact with teammates and coaching staff? How does he prepare his body to compete?

PRO TIP: College coaches and scouts no longer focus on radar readings in a showcase or bullpen. Instead, they prefer to wait for the lights and score board to be turned on. Game time matters, so be ready to compete!

Health

Most college coaches and scouts will ask student-athletes or their coaches if a pitcher has any current or previous injury, or a history of recent surgeries or health concerns. Having an injury doesn't mean an athlete will not be considered a prospect; it simply allows coaches to have a history of a student-athlete. Always be honest and up front when asked about health history. Strength and conditioning programs started early in an athlete's career will always lead to a strong foundation for a healthy career.

What Do College Baseball Scouts Look for in a Catcher?

Tool Breakdown by Role Value at Catcher

1. Power
2. Catching Ability
3. Hitting Ability
4. Throwing Ability
5. Running Ability/Speed

Statistical Breakdown Beyond College

What was once a receiving and throwing position has become a power-first position. The catchers of years past could rifle the ball and you would rarely see anything less than an average Major League arm that was quick and accurate. Important, relevant stats for the position are fielding percentage, framing statistics, passed balls, and an ERA below 3.00 for your pitchers.

Defensive Ability

The defensive role of a catcher is one of the most important on the diamond. Defensive excellence is a notable generator of pride among backstops. Today, catchers are judged by their ability to receive and throw. When asked to throw out an attempted base-stealer, the throw must be accurate and in the 2.0-second range from release to catch (mitt to mitt). This is pop time.

PRO TIP: Be accurate and realistic with your pop times. Coaches don't want "fish stories." Look up MLB averages. If you are posting pop times for your 15-year-old that are similar to the best in the game, it calls into question *all* your metrics.

Game calling, blocking ability, and leadership are all still attributes all MLB personnel want as part of the player's overall package. Fielding percentage as a catcher and thrown-out percentage are still defensive measuring sticks for ability and overall position worth.

Offensive Breakdown

Today's catchers, if showing any offensive capabilities, are judged by their home run production. College coaches and pro scouts are looking for present size and strength at the catching position. A middle of the order bat is a huge bonus, and a solid offensive contributor will be followed aggressively by MLB scouts. Any high school catchers who are above average defensively and show an ability to make consistent hard contact at the plate will certainly be a strongly recruited student-athlete.

OFP Breakdown

By overall future potential the catching position is considered the least talented in baseball. The best catchers in today's game—Salvatore Perez, Mike Zunino, and JT Realmuto—are considered strong two-way caliber catchers. Many college and professional catchers are limited offensively. Platoons at both the college and professional levels are common. So a catcher who has both offensive tools and receiving ability has a chance to be an all-star at the position.

- Coaches will take a closer look at catching and throwing mechanics as well as the arm strength shown while throwing to second and third base.
- While defense comes first for a catcher, NCAA Division 1 coaches will also look for a player who demonstrates outstanding leadership skills and who can work with the entire pitching staff.
- Catchers swing the bat well and usually can hit for power or average at an elevated level.

Age	Catcher Pop Time			Catcher Velocity		
	Average	Plus	Elite	Average	Plus	Elite
14U	2.20	1.98	1.98	68	73	75
15U	2.12	1.96	1.91	71	76	79
16U	2.16	1.94	1.89	73	78	80
17U	2.01	1.90	1.84	75	79	82

What Do College Baseball Scouts Look for in a First Baseman?

Coaches look for offensive tools first at first base. It is a corner position bat, meaning they want a good combination of power and average:

- Usually hits 3–6 in a college batting order
- Power bat
- Preferably a left-handed hitter
- Ability to drive in runs and hit for average

Tool Breakdown by Role Value at First Base

1. Power
2. Hit Ability
3. Fielding Ability
4. Arm Strength
5. Running Ability/Speed

Statistical Breakdown Beyond College

We're still looking for a corner position bat, someone who can hit 3–6 in an MLB order, and preferably a left-handed hitter. On-base percentage (OBP), OBP + slugging (OPS), and total bases are key indicators for high-achieving corner position bats.

First basemen will hit for average and power. Most MLB first basemen will hit for a .275 average and 30+ home runs per season.

Defensive Breakdown

Most MLB first basemen take pride in their defense prowess. Many become high-level defenders. Saving runs and minimizing damage by their ability to control errant throws, the first baseman's skill as a defender can elevate him to being an elite player because he has carrying tools on both sides of the ball. Arm strength and speed are not as important for this position. Hands and the ability to receive are a must after the ability to hit for power and average

Offensive Breakdown

Scouts want an aggressive hitter that has a dominant tool in hitting ability or power. Left-handed bats are always at a premium. Players such as Freddie Freeman, Matt Olsen, and Vlad Guerrero Jr are examples of the type of offensive players that scouts are seeking.

OFP Breakdown

A 60 OFP grade or better is preferred at this position—someone who will be an all-star player in his best years. The bat tools at first base are the predominant tools when being graded by college coaches and MLB scouts. It's a middle-of-the-order type of bat that knocks runners in off the bases or hits baseballs over the fence. Aa strong grade offensively for a starting first baseman at the high school or college level indicates advanced upside in power and hitting for average.

What Do College Baseball Scouts Look for in a Second Baseman?

Tool Breakdown by Role Value at Second Base

1. Power
2. Hit Ability
3. Fielding Ability
4. Speed
5. Arm Strength

Statistical Breakdown Beyond College

High-scoring second basemen are dotted all over MLB lineups. Most second basemen will hit for around a .270 average. The position has become a power breeding ground for superstar type players, with the top players scoring 30+ home runs per year.

Defensive Breakdown

Most MLB second basemen are efficient and fast turning the double play. With shifts being used, you will get a truer sense of their arm strength. Most are sure handed and can move and throw from various arm angles. You don't have to have the strongest arm to play the position, but you do have to have a quick release and accurate arm. Backhand and slow roller plays also define a second baseman's overall defensive ability.

Offensive Breakdown

This position, just as much as any, has transformed into a power hitting position at the MLB level in recent years. Possessing strong athletic ability, these players usually hit towards the top of lineup. You will occasionally see them occupy the 3-hole slot. It has become a very offensively focused position. It is important to note that the skilled offensive shortstop who may lack necessary arm strength will always have a position at second base. It is becoming a premium offensive position at both the college and pro levels.

OFP Breakdown

It's interesting that many international players and college draftees make up the position in high numbers. Many high school players drafted at shortstop then eventually moved because the skill set just profiles better at second base. For championship teams, we are always trying to have 60-graded players all over the field. The dominant tool of power will get OFP in the range where it needs to be to make the player have value.

What Do College Baseball Scouts Look for in a Third Baseman?

Tool Breakdown by Role Value at Third Base

1. Power
2. Hitting Ability
3. Fielding Ability
4. Arm Strength
5. Speed

Statistical Breakdown Beyond College

Third base is an offensively focused, corner bat position. The player usually hits 3–6 in the order. Most third basemen will hit 25+ home runs and be in the .260–.280 range for average. A 60 OFP grade for power and 55 OFP for average equals most times a potential all-star player. Value increases with fielding tools and how elite players can become, known as upside.

Defensive Breakdown

It's not every day that you get Gold Glove–type defense like a Manny Machado. Machado can make every play for the position and his range and arm strength only make him more of a premium type of player. Defensively, the most common footwork is a one-step-and-dive position, with more value placed on players that can make the slow roller play.

Most third basemen are gifted with Strong to Plus arms. Scouts always want a player that can handle the routine ball. They want that player whose defense doesn't cost you runs. Versatile and agile players on this corner carry great defensive value.

Offensive Breakdown

Third basemen show the ability to hit the ball out of the park. Guys like Austin Riley, Manny Machado, Rafael Devers and Justin Turner are players that can be your power run producers in your lineup as 3–6-hole hitters. Any time you can get 30+ home runs and hit .270 and above, you're looking at a player who will play in All-Star games. They will strike out more than most, but will also score runs and knock in runs. Predominantly more right-handed hitters, the value in the position lies in offensive production.

OFP Breakdown

A 60 as a Plus prospect will always get this player drafted in the first round. Third base, as much as any position, is a tough position to find. The biggest key when drafting this position is power—raw power—and the ability to defend. Some may grade the position as defense being Average with hit ability Plus. It's difficult to find everything scouts want in this position. There are a limited number of players who have every tool. Some have two tools but don't hold all three main tools for the position. Those with all three will have long careers and be very valuable to their team. Also, defenders like Machado and Matt Chapman (a three-tool player) affect the game defensively with their ability to make plays.

Defensive ability can elevate players in final rankings by position and in Final OFP-Offensive Numbers (meaning, that player's OFP when you take offense out of the equation).

What Do College Baseball Scouts Look for in a Shortstop?

Tool Breakdown by Role Value at Shortstop

1. Hitting Ability
2. Fielding Ability
3. Arm Strength
4. Power
5. Running Ability

Statistical Breakdown Beyond College

This is your premium middle infield position. (Premium means it's a position of highest value, along with centerfield, catcher, and left-handed pitchers.) Usually the shortstop is the best player on the field. They are well-rounded athletes who show an abundance of tools, not limited to:

- Fielding Percentage: the number of chances that are converted without making an error
- Plus/Minus: how many runs a fielder saves (or gives away) over the average fielder

Defensive Breakdown

Shortstops are typically the most-athletic player on the team, or at least the player with the best combination of foot speed, quickness, throwing and fielding abilities. Shortstops also need a strong arm so they can be an effective cut-off man as well as make the longest throws from the 5–6 hole on back hand plays. The three things if broken down to the core of the position and being able to play it would be footwork, mechanics, and angles. Players, through data, have become so much better positioned to better utilize their abundance of skills and natural physical gifts. Most shortstops have above average instincts and game awareness. It's just a total feel for the game.

Offensive Breakdown

Shortstops on most teams carry the burden of having to be able to do it on both sides of the ball. Usually considered the most gifted, best athletes on the field, it's not every day that you see a shortstop that can combine hitting ability and power in the same package. Today's shortstops—the Fernando Tatis Jr's, Francisco Lindor's and Carlos Correia's—all play a huge part in the success of their respective teams and usually hit third in the batting order. The 3-hole hitter is responsible for being the most dominant and consistent hitting player in your team, wants the biggest moments of the game hitting, and sometimes can be the one player that elevates the players around them. Some shortstops have the ability to hit 40+ home runs, but most are 18–25 home run–type hitters with the ability to hit a .260–.280 average.

MVP candidates come from this position.

OFP Breakdown

Many of today's shortstops' play and value has been elevated because of the power numbers they are putting up. Their run production justifies the chance of getting a 60 OFP grade or better. We're looking for a potential MVP candidate. A 50 OFP is a very productive player that offensively doesn't hit or hit for power better than .250–.260 average and 17–23 home runs. These are solid contributions, but scouts are always looking for better. A 40 OFP is an end-of-the-roster player that has value because he can help defensively as a utility player or with his late-game defensive ability.

What Do College Baseball Scouts Look for in a Corner Outfielder?

Tool Breakdown by Role Value at Corner Outfield

1. Power
2. Hit Ability
3. Defensive Ability
4. Arm Strength
5. Speed

Statistical Breakdown Beyond College

Your corner outfield position has evolved into "if you don't hit, you won't play." Corner outfielders excel in the power and hit abilities, and ideally you want a corner outfielder with a .900 OPS or higher. You'd like the position to hit 3–5 in your batting order and be the player that hits home runs. You'd like a consistent defender that doesn't cost your pitching staff pitches because the position lacks range or judgment and instincts.

Defensive Breakdown

Ideally you want defenders at all positions. Defense in a corner outfield position is not one of the requirements of the position that holds higher value. You'd like a player that exhibits Average tools in the field, not all Below

Averages. Right field is more of an arm strength position; left field is more about accuracy, knowing how to get to the throw, and being precise in throwing to the right bases. You would like both defenders to make routine plays look routine. Still, in the end you want hitters in left field and right field. Late-in-game defenders for defensive purposes can be substituted in. Make the routine play. Make smart decisions. Don't cost your team and pitchers extra pitches.

Offensive Breakdown

Your corner outfield bats hopefully combine power and high average. You need production from these two positions for your team to have success. Corner bats ideally hit .275 or greater in a lineup. Potential power numbers represent value to the team. Left-handed hitting is always an obvious plus.

OFP Breakdown

At this position more than any you need thumpers—big bat potential. These are middle-of-the-order hitters, run producers, and power and high average hitters. Teams that possess strong offensive players in their corner outfield positions are often top tier teams or programs. Possessing other tools and playing ability at the position obviously makes the player greater in value. Superstars occupy these positions (an all-star type of ability). Teams' ability to win games and championships are largely due to the production of corner position players.

What do college baseball scouts look for in a Centerfielder?

Tool Breakdown by Role Value at Centerfield

1. Hitting Ability
2. Defensive Ability
3. Power
4. Speed
5. Arm Strength

Statistical Breakdown Beyond College

Obviously defensive metrics for the position high on the food chain of ability. These guys usually have speed and instincts in their tool sets. Centerfielders are potential leadoff hitters as well as 3-hole hitters in your lineups. They should have all-star ability and perform in All-Star games throughout their career. Centerfielders are typically considered one of the two best athletes on the field.

Defensive Breakdown

It's a position played by people that are instinctive, usually possess speed, and are just above average to excellent defenders. They're playmakers, whether catching the ball or at times throwing the baseball. An accurate arm is more important than strength arm, but arm strength will be seen from this position as well. You'd like to have enough speed to go gap to gap.

Offensive Breakdown

This position over the years has evolved to an offensive player first. They will be high average hitters over power production. The elite, top-of-the-game centerfielders will give you both Power and Average: these guys will be graded 70 OFP or better as hitters. A .300 average is not uncommon for this position. Power numbers are 17+ home runs on the norm, but you will have that all-star performer who can do it all offensively.

OFP Breakdown

A grade of 60 OFP is the norm at this position. A second-tier centerfielder will be 55 OFP and above, and backup-type players at this position will carry the 50 OFP tag as an average MLB player. Superstars will be at this position, especially if they have an OPS over 1.000. Value is value, and centerfielders carry huge value; they're another position that is important to a team's success from both an offensive and defensive standpoint.

Keep Working

Student-athletes, keep working and trust the process. I (Butch) scouted Aaron Judge when he was a high school player in Linden, CA, and turned him in as a second– or third-round type player. Many scouts had Judge as a guy that needed to go to college. Some guys that came to see him didn't like him as a player. Judge went to Fresno State, became the player my eyes had seen three years earlier, and the rest is history.

Keep working.

THE DECISION PROCESS

It is important for all parents and student-athletes to understand that this process is unique for each prospective student-athlete. Be sure to weigh all the information about a prospective college or university to ensure that your crucial criteria and priorities, and as many as possible, of important needs and wants, including your student-athletes' academic, social, family and financial needs (and not just the athletic ones) are met.

When I begin to work with families, I try to make sure that they understand that this is a forty-year decision. It is NOT only about four years of baseball.

In addition to the more obvious topics, some families I have helped over the last 30 years include have felt these were important areas to consider as well:

- Does a student-athlete want a major metropolitan city or more of a rural environment?
- How close is the cafeteria to the dorm?
- Where is the library located as it relates to the dorms as well as the baseball facility?
- How far are the dorms in relation to the athletic facilities?
- What is the undergraduate student population on campus?

This is not simply a baseball decision; it's a life altering choice. Don't fear the choice, but embrace it by being the most informed you can be. Friendships and relationships made during the college years last a lifetime. Future spouse, job connections, and permanent residence often happen because of the decision about where one chooses to attend college.

In this chapter I provide a questionnaire that will guide the decision process. The student-athlete should fill it out themselves. As I said in "The Road Ahead," this is *their* choice. Put some real thought into the answers.

Maybe even answer the questions and, before making any plans, let the answers sit for a week or two; revisit them to make sure none of the answers were given in an emotional or uninformed state. I have intentionally given plenty of blank lines to use.

The only wrong answers are ones that do not genuinely reflect the priorities of the prospective student-athlete. Mom and Dad, this is a tough intersection. I know because I wanted to go through it with my two sons whom I love deeply. Giving them the space to learn to be their own young adult self is important for their development and your future relationship. Be a resource; don't be the instigator or the decider.

Students, I strongly encourage you to write in and mark up the book, as it then becomes your personal workbook to refer to throughout the decision process.

Questions you will want to work through include (but are not limited to):

- What makes a NJCAA/JUCO school better than an NCAA Division 3 program?
- Could an NCAA Division 2 program be a better fit than a Division 1 program?
- How do you make those choices?

For me, it comes down to three primary focal points:

1. What type of academic transcript (AP, Honors, or CP level courses, and GPA, plus the standardized test scores, if any) will a student present to an admissions office?

2. What is a student-athlete's athletic ability level and their desire and drive to improve? Each player must have a firm understanding and evaluation of their athletic ability both from self-evaluation and getting an outside evaluation. It is especially important to not overestimate or sell yourself short. Talk to people with no personal stake, but lots of experience in accurately assessing young players for projectability; it may take some time to find these people but know they are out there. Later in this book are several people who are available for potentially giving you their targeted skill assessments. (It is obviously up to each of them as to whether they can help you; it is intended to be a resource

for your family to have a jumping-off point for getting good information and insight).

3. Is the student-athlete truly driven to be part of a college baseball program? It takes 24-40 hours a week of workouts and practices. Understand that a typical day is up at 5am and ends after a study hall at 10-11pm. It makes for a long day for most student-athletes.

What I am saying is that there is not one single recipe for success. There is no script or blueprint to follow. Each student-athlete must make an individual decision based on their unique qualifications. The one common thread that all student-athletes have in common is a desire to play beyond high school.

With that in mind, the priority is to find a college program that wants you, and that you want to attend. Let me say that again…*wants you*. Go to a place that fits you and really appreciates what you can bring to the program and school. Doing so means you have a quicker path to real playing time, and that is priceless. What good are you doing yourself besides stroking your ego if you are riding the pine for three (or more!) years. Go to where you have your best fit and where you are going to play.

Remember, too, the no's are just as important as the yes's. Get an idea of your likes and dislikes, your wants and needs, and your priorities. This helps you narrow your focus and refine your list. You are the athlete, not mom or dad. You are the ones that have to live with your choices. With over 30 years of experience coaching and guiding student-athletes (including my two sons), the following is the exact tool I use with them, sitting at my kitchen table with our favorite takeout in front of us. Take your time and mark up often! The more you write the better! You should refer to this workbook often. Do not be afraid to change any answer and course correct as you make progress through your process. The odds are good you might change your mind about some things, and that is OK.

Let's not start from a 20,000-foot viewpoint, meaning too broad a focus. Instead of being overwhelmed with all the options that are possible, let's narrow our focus to what's important to your athlete and family. Just like if you were looking at buying a new house or car, getting clear on both what we do want and what we don't want is the best place to start.

Let us start with making a don't list. Write down everything you can think of that you don't want (i.e., I do not want to sit on the bench the entire year, I do not want to be in a cold climate, I do not want to be in a big school, etc.) Make sure you get all the small things as well!

_____

_____

_____

_____

_____

_____

_____

_____

Now, let us flip the script and make a do list. Write down *everything* you can think of that you do want (i.e., I want to have supportive coaches, I want to play as much as possible, I want to have great training facilities, etc.) Again, make sure you get all the small things as well.

Now that we have a good idea of what you do and don't want, let us get a little more detail on some specifics that you may or may not have thought of.

Student Athlete Questionnaire

Geography Matters

When considering a school, do you want to go further or far away from home. How far? Is it important for you to be able to have your family come watch you play? Do Sunday home dinners matter to you?

_____

_____

_____

_____

_____

_____

_____

_____

_____

What Kind of Weather Do You Prefer to Live in and Play in?

It's not uncommon for players to wilt in heat and humidity and stiffen in the cold. So, by prefer, I mean what climates do you *excel* at playing in? Many coaches prefer to only recruit players from their areas and climates, but not all do. Do your research and you can find those coaches that have stated their preferences; sometimes you can get this information by reading the hometowns of the players on their current roster. Coach Corbin at Vanderbilt, for example, does not only recruit from the south. He loves to recruit from the New England area as he sees a certain toughness out of those players. Most of those players have acclimated to playing in the cold. The opposite is also true. Some coaches from hot climates feel they need to recruit players who are already used to playing in extreme heat. Think it through and answer at length.

_____

_____

_____

_____

_____

_____

_____

_____

_____

School Size/Location (City or Country)/Diversity/Culture

Do you know yourself well enough to know if you think you might prefer a big campus to a small one? Small class sizes vs. lecture hall settings? Many large campuses are spread out over a lot of land, so check on how undergraduates get around to classes (bus or train systems, shuttles, walking or biking, etc.). When would you be able to bring a car? What environment would be most comfortable for you?

_____

_____

_____

_____

_____

_____

_____

_____

City Versus Rural Areas

Some schools are very remote, without a lot of outside distractions. Some in-town settings tend to be the only entertainment. The thought process here is again what lifestyle I feel will best help me become the best student-athlete I can be. Am I easily distracted? Do I manage time well in the quiet? Do I really do better with hustle and bustle around me? For some, city noises can be soothing, but for others it can be overwhelming. Is proximity to activities off campus important to me? Or is it important to have a lot of options for culture and entertainment on the weekends? Or, even, proximity to family?

_____

_____

_____

_____

_____

_____

_____

_____

_____

PRO TIP: Use the map and search features on the NCAA Membership Directory to find schools. https://www.ncaa.org/sports/2021/5/3/membership-directory.aspx

What Is the Campus Social Life Like?

Is it mostly a commuter school (where most of campus goes home on the weekends)? Are fraternities and sororities a part of campus life? Do other sports excel there? Are there other teams to go watch and root for? Are there intramural programs or other student activities to participate in? And, if there are, will the coaches support it if it's important to me (student government, Bible studies, semester abroad, etc.)? Are there service requirements, or community involvement opportunities? How involved in the outside community is the school? (Note: If a university is the one of the top two or three employers in a city/town, the odds are good that much of the life of the community will be tied to the health of the athletic department.)

Is social, cultural, economic diversity important to you? Do you want to meet and learn about people from different parts of the U.S. and the world? Is attending a school with a strong religious heritage important to you? Or do you prefer one with a secular approach? Keep in mind the more diverse a school is, it's likely to offer a more well-rounded education: I believe everyone grows and develops better when they realize there are unique differences all around the world and embrace learning new things. Yes, that even means it helps you on the ball field! Being open to new teaching styles and coaching methods, and being coachable, starts with being open to learning new things.

_____

_____

_____

_____

_____

_____

_____

_____

_____

Academic Rigor

What is the SAT or ACT requirement, or is there one? Many schools (due to the impacts of COVID) have either temporarily or permanently waived the SAT as an entrance requirement. This is a huge deal. If you are a good, standardized test taker, it can really set you apart. If you are not, then not needing to take a test can help you. Know your strengths and lean into them. It is critical, however, for you to know early in the process each school's admission requirements (the minimum) and recommendations (what they want to see). This will include assessing where your SAT (or ACT) score fits in relationship to the schools' published 75/25 range (i.e., if a school's 75/25 range is 1100-1250, that means that 25% of admitted students score less than 1100 and 25% score above 1250).

I always advise a student-athlete to take the SAT (or ACT) at least twice after taking test prep extra, because you just never know how you'll do until you take the test (after really trying to do well) … or … or choose from among the schools for your list that don't require one. Don't let something as simple as preparing for the SAT (or ACT) to be the thing that keeps you from playing the game you love for a few more years.

Choice of Majors

Does the school offer your preferred major(s)? Does the difficulty of the major you see yourself pursuing affect the level you are hoping to play at? For example, it may be a big ask (of yourself, your teammates, and your coaches) if you are considering pre-med while also going to a Power 5 school. It's also something to ask the coaches when you visit with them. [NOTE: This is also covered in the section on questions to ask during visits.]

_____

_____

_____

_____

_____

_____

_____

_____

Are the Service Academies, Ivy League, or Near Ivies a possibility?

Please see my description of some of the aspects of these schools for further info. Even if you can qualify academically and emotionally to attend, it's okay to say no. If you do choose an academy, thank you in advance for your service.

_____

_____

_____

_____

_____

_____

_____

_____

_____

Cost

What tuition range, after grants and loans, that myself and my family will be responsible for, do we need to stay in?

_____

Questions Specific to The Baseball Programs

I prioritized these based on what I recommend you ask first and what you ask last. These are mostly questions you should consider when researching schools and programs.

How is the roster put together? Where do most players come from? How important does the physical size of the players seem to be to the staff? How many players are on the roster? How many fifth-year players are there? (This is super important in 2022 and 2023, but will be less important the further we get away from the one-time eligibility decisions the NCAA made in the middle of the COVID lockdowns.) What are the graduation rates? Make notes here after researching the answers to these questions online.

_____

_____

_____

_____

_____

_____

What is your skill set? Does the playing style of the program match your skill set?

What are their philosophies regarding pitching? You can see how many pitches a game they ask their pitchers to throw, and you can determine if they set their players up to get through school with a healthy arm, or if they are overusing their best pitchers (increasing the odds of injury). Do they subscribe to a specific training and development method?

Coach Vaughn at Maryland made a great point at a showcase event I once attended. If you're a pitcher who's trained for years in a certain manner or system that you want to continue using, and you choose a school whose pitching coach is strongly opposed to that, then you will forever be butting heads and miserable. And butting heads with the pitching coach will only make it harder to earn innings on the mound. Coach Vaughn said those things absolutely matter and should be discussed during the recruiting process. Also, as a pitcher, you should want to know how much emphasis the recruiting staff places on finding guys who know what to do with that glove on their hand.

For you position players, what kind of hitters are they looking for on the offensive side? Power guys, gap to gap, speed specialists? Do they like versatility in their players? This is not to say you could not and should not adapt, but to get quality playing time sooner it's better to be a match in as many ways as you can. This is where you want to be sure you are not trying to fit a square peg into a round hole.

Skipping these questions about skill set and skill set fit can lead to substantial amounts of conflict and discontent. Not accurately assessing this ahead of time is the number one cause of a player deciding to transfer before their eligibility is exhausted. Further, development is slowed if the player does not match—or want to try and match—the system.

PRO TIP: Learn to be versatile. Be willing to try everything necessary to get on the field. Self-Assess your game, know who you are as a player now, and know where you need to make improvements.

Versatility is king!

How important is it to you that you get on the field right away? The obvious answer should be as early as possible. If it is not, that is okay, but you must know why it isn't your first priority. It may be you love the academic side of the school so much that you are willing to sacrifice playing time in return for a great education that stretches the limits of your academic abilities. That's fantastic.

If that isn't the reason, you need to be honest with yourself. Is it because you want the name on the jersey to make a splash on social media, or with friends or family? Many times, the flashier the name the longer the wait to get the playing time you could have somewhere else. If that is the reason, then you need to be okay with seeing very limited time for most of your college career. You are not the only one who will want to go to Famous University for the prestige of doing so. For those of you with goals of playing professionally, going to a big-name school might not be the best way to get there. What good is wearing the cool uniform if it never gets dirty?

_____

_____

_____

_____

_____

Does the age of the staff matter? You should want to know how long some of the staff have been around. You should ask how many assistant coaches are paid and how many are volunteer, what their roles are, and how they will help you as an athlete, as a student and as a person on the brink of adulthood.

_____

_____

_____

_____

_____

How important to you is the use of technology within the program? What technology do they use on and off the field to help you succeed and develop your game? What value does a program place on using tech? Will you own your own data should you decide to transfer? Will they invest in you to be the best you, or try to make you fit inside their box, come hell or high water?

_____

_____

_____

_____

_____

How do you want to spend your summers? Do you want to participate in MLB development programs? Most NCAA Division 1 programs require their players to participate in a collegiate summer league. A lot of times those students spend summers closer to school than to home. So, find out what the schools you are interested in have in mind for your summers.

_____

_____

_____

_____

_____

What support systems are in place for student-athletes? Are there mandatory study halls? Is academic tutoring available? Does the school have strong (and readily available) mental health resources? Playing a sport in college can be stressful. You will be maintaining grades, competing for playing time, acclimating to a new environment that first year, dealing with the difficulties of romantic relationships, and possibly overcoming injuries at times. Make sure the schools you are considering can really help you should you ever need it. Do not shortchange this. Your life may very well rest on it.

_____

_____

_____

_____

_____

How important are the training facilities and their quality to you? Is a strong medical and training staff important to you? Nutrition and weight room support? What type of surface does the program play on? Do you care? How is the mound maintained? The warning track? Does the dugout face into the sun? How close-in are the fences? Where will you throw bullpens and take batting practice?

PRO TIP: DO NOT ask questions about how much gear you will get or who will be the sponsors. DO NOT ASK THAT QUESTION! Besides, if you look at pictures of the players, you will know the answer to the sponsorship question.

Using Your Questionnaire

These questions are word-for-word what I have used at my kitchen table for the many athletes I have helped over the decades. They help them see the trees among forest of schools out there, navigate the decision process, and lay out at least the first draft of the list of schools they should begin to contact. You can do this on your own or with the help of your parents or a mentor.

Make sure the first draft of your list is limited to no more than 30 schools. These should be evenly distributed across every level of opportunity: all three NCAA divisions, NAIA, JUCO, and post-graduate.

Lay out a spreadsheet to track all the details you collect. Clearly label everything so you can keep track of contact information, the answers to your questions, and any other information or changes you uncover along the way. Order this spreadsheet by school preference. It will be extremely helpful during your decision-making process to have this information quickly available.

The online app The Baseball Bluebook is a great resource for finding the most current information to fill out your spreadsheet. Use it to gather information, but not as a place to store that info. Maintaining a personal spreadsheet keeps your list focused on *your* needs and wants. Using online sources to store your info can become too much of a distraction and lead you to think way too broadly. You want to keep the list of choices tight, throwing out some and replacing them with others as needed.

It's also helpful to use a recruiting service's profile system to get contact info, send emails, share links to videos, etc. I will get into the pros and cons of such services in the chapter "Your Recruiting Roadmap." For now, focus on using the questionnaire to determine your best fit.

Transfer Portal Tsunami

It used to be that if a student-athlete wanted to transfer schools they had to ask their coach's permission. There were a number of steps that would happen after that before the student could transfer.

That all changed in 2018 when the NCAA changed its bylaws and allowed students-athletes to start the transfer process on their own. At the same time, the NCAA launched an online transfer portal for tracking the students looking to transfer. Now all a student-athlete has to do is fill out the right forms and submit them to the compliance administrator at their school. Within two days, the whole world of college athletics knows they are looking to transfer. The process is easier than it used to be. It's so easy that many student-athletes and parents think if they don't like the school they pick or if things don't work there, that it's an easy fix to transfer. It's not that simple.

Bloated rosters, limited money, coaching changes, and the ease of initiating a transfer has led to what I call the transfer portal tsunami. Then you must consider all the JUCO students looking to continue their academic and athletic careers at a 4-year school, students from lower divisions seeking better programs…there is a massive wave of student-athletes looking to find a better fit. Once you enter the transfer portal, you are another drop of water in that wave. You are competing against all of those student-athletes for a roster spot and scholarship. It's a big version of musical chairs, and there are a lot more academically dedicated and athletically skilled students out there than you may think.

So control what you can control, which is how prepared you are to make a decision you'll be satisfied with for four years.

COLLEGES' RECRUTING ROADMAP

The NCAA has created a recruiting calendar that spells out, in exact detail

- When and how a program and its staff can make contact or be contacted by an athlete,
- At what age they can start creating a relationship,
- When a school can even begin to say a word about even having an interest in an athlete, and
- What year they can make an offer official or even make just a verbal offer.

These restrictions exist for two reasons. They create fairness among NCAA schools when it comes to competing for student-athletes, and they give you time to make a good, patient decision.

PRO TIP: Get to know the recruiting calendars and guides for the three NCAA divisions. They are available at https://www.ncaa.org/sports/2018/5/8/division-i-and-ii-recruiting-calendars.aspx

---

At What Age Do College Coaches Begin to Look at Student Athletes?

As I mentioned earlier, coaches begin looking at prospects as soon as they are physically developed enough to give a reliable estimation of how they will project as an 18– to 21-year-old player. Usually, this is when the student is in their sophomore or junior year of high school. In rare instances it happens at age 14, but the projections usually come into focus more clearly after age 15.

Projecting an athlete is difficult and coaches take different approaches to projecting players. Some coaches are willing to project earlier than others, and athletes develop on different timelines. Prospects looking to get recruited cannot control when they develop or what coaches think of them. Regardless of your age, prospects should focus on getting better and putting themselves in the right position against the best competition available. As I have said repeatedly, those student-athletes who focus on their strength and physical development starting at 13–14 will clearly be ahead of their peers that have yet to begin a strength and conditioning program.

PRO TIP: Focus resources and finances on an exceptionally good strength and conditioning trainer during early years rather than just skill set work (i.e., hitting/pitching).

Periods on the Recruiting Calendar

Now we'll get into the when and how of contact. In its Division 1 manual, NCAA defines contact as "any face-to-face encounter…during which dialogue occurs in excess of an exchange of a greeting."

- **Contact period**. Coaches and recruits are allowed to communicate with the least restrictions: phone, email, campus contact, or off-campus contact.
- **Evaluation period**. A coach can watch a recruit compete in a game but cannot talk to them face-to-face.
- **Dead period**. Coaches are not allowed to have any communication with recruits other than talking to them on the phone or writing to them. Evaluations/scouting off campus is not allowed.
- **Quiet period**. This is when coaches are not allowed to meet with recruits or scout off-campus, but they are allowed to meet with recruits who come to campus.

All three NCAA divisions are also restricted on when in high school they can start contacting you. Those restrictions are not only about creating a level playing field. They are in place for your benefit, so that you have the time to make a good decision about where you want to attend school.

Division 1 Contact

Contact can't begin until September 1 of your junior year of high school.

The 2022–23 Division 1 recruiting calendar for baseball is available at https://ncaaorg.s3.amazonaws.com/compliance/recruiting/calendar/2022-23/2022-23D1Rec_MBARecruitingCalendar.pdf. The dates are listed below:

- August 1–14, 2022. Contact period.
- August 15–September 8, 2022. Quiet period.
- September 9–October 9. Contact period.
- October 10, 2022–February 28, 2023. Quiet period, except for dead periods November 7–10, 2022, and January 5–8, 2023.
- March 1 through July 31, 2023. Contact period, except for dead periods May 29–June 5, June 17–19, and July 3–5, 2023.

Division 2 Contact

Contact can begin June 15 before your junior year of high school. Depending on where you live, you may still be in your sophomore year at that time.

The 2022–23 Divison 2 recruting calendar is available at https://ncaaorg.s3.amazonaws.com/compliance/recruiting/calendar/2022-23/2022-23D2REC_RecCalendars_SOTFB.pdf.

The 48-hour dead period on the Division 2 recruiting calendar matches up with the National Letter of Intent (NLI) initial signing day. Whichever year you're in, look up that date. The dead period begins at 7 a.m. two days before the initial signing day and ends at 7 a.m. the morning of the initial signing day. For 2022, that makes the dead period from 7 a.m. on November 7 to 7 a.m. on November 9. The coach may write or telephone during this period. Any date outside of the dead period is within the contact period.

NCAA Division 3, NAIA, and NJCAA Contact

NCAA Division 3, NAIA, and NJCAA do not have any dead or quiet periods; their contact period is all year.

- In NCAA Division 3, contact cannot start until you've completed your sophomore year of high school.
- NAIA schools have no limits on when contact can start.
- JUCO schools can contact you as long as you've not signed a junior college letter of intent. They have no limits on when contact can start.

Athletic Scholarships

Discussions about athletic scholarships happen toward the end of the recruiting process. Baseball is vastly different from football and basketball in that *very few schools can offer a full-ride athletic scholarship*. This is another reason to have a great GPA and transcript full of advanced courses. Schools can make up for that lack of athletic money with academic money! Remember, the coaches want to keep their jobs and so want to do everything they can to have the highest number of the best players on their team by whatever means necessary. Academics can be your carrying tool that separates you from similar players.

Here is the breakdown for each division on *their* eligibility to offer scholarships:

- **NCAA Division 1** may award the equivalent of 11.7 athletic scholarships; the minimum athletic scholarship is 25% of tuition. As you learned in "The Options," not all schools award athletic scholarships.
- **NCAA Division 2** may award the equivalent of 9 athletic scholarships. There's no minimum, and not all schools award athletic scholarships.
- **NCAA Division 3** is not allowed to offer athletic scholarships. Student-athletes should investigate the academic scholarships available at the schools they are considering.
- **NJCAA Divisions 1, 2, and 3** athletic scholarships vary by school and programs.
  - NJCAA Division 1—24 full-tuition scholarships plus room & board (or $400 for living expenses)
  - NJCAA Division 2—24 full tuition scholarships
  - NJCAA Division 3—Only academic money
- **NAIA Divisions 1 and 2** have basically two sets of scholarship systems. Most are eligible to award 12 full athletic scholarships as well as academic scholarships for (spring) competition.
  - Academic funds available to continuing students. Full aid is available to students with a 3.6–4.0 cumulative GPA. Half aid is available to students with a 3.3–3.59 cumulative GPA.
  - Academic funds available to incoming students. Full aid is available to students with a 3.75–4.0 GPA, 1270 SAT, 27 ACT, or who are in the top 10 percent of their class. Half aid is available to students

with a 3.50–3.74 GPA, 1130 SAT, 23 ACT, or who are in the top 11–25 percent of their class.

Very rarely do programs have a student-athlete on a full scholarship because of limitations on what each school distributes for scholarship money. Schools can combine academic and athletic scholarships, but that is not the case at every school.

PRO TIP: Anything you can do to raise your academic profile (e.g., raising your core course GPA) will directly lead to more money from the school you end up attending. It may dramatically impact the quality of the school you can attend. While every school is limited in athletic scholarship money, and some cannot give any athletic scholarships, they all find a way to give academic money. Don't leave that on the table!

YOUR RECRUITING ROADMAP

Neither the calendar nor the recruiting rules address what's called the coach's loophole. There's no requirement for a coach to follow through on the offers and promises made to high school student-athletes. As you use the tools and information in this book to work through your process, never lose sight of that. It's a major reason it is imperative that both the student-athlete and parent create an open, real, truthful, and strong relationship with the head coach *and* the recruiting coordinator for each program that they are interested in. Consistent communication is necessary, so that you can get a realistic feel for:

- How great the interest is on their end
- How truthful and straightforward they are being with you

A good thing to do is to talk to your baseball family and community about their experiences with that program. Find out the good and the bad. You want to know it all from multiple sources and different angles, ex-assistants, players, other recruits, etc.

The baseball community is small and getting smaller. Everyone talks. You just need to ask questions and listen…just listen.

As you move forward in this chapter, we will try to add clarity and direction to beginning the contact with coaches. We'll also try to help with how to develop relationships with coaches in those programs that you have determined may be a good fit.

What Do You Need to Do to Get Recruited by College Baseball Coaches?

Some say talented players will be found, but the numbers and facts just don't bear that out. There are mountains of amazing ball players out there. Student-athletes *cannot* count on a college coach finding them. They must be proactive in communicating with coaches and diligent in following up. Otherwise, chances are they will not be on a coach's radar when it comes to identifying recruits to evaluate.

After lengthy discussions with hundreds of college baseball coaches, most begin aggressively evaluating recruits in their sophomore and junior years of high school. Tournaments, showcases, and camps are the major sources of recruits. Get coaches' eyes on you during these years.

Student-athletes who show accountability for their own recruiting process immediately show a commitment to their individual process. This is a great separator in the eyes of college coaches.

Your Recruiting Toolbox

Before you contact coaches you should build your recruiting toolbox. Make your skills video, get it out there, sign up with recruiting services so you can start publicizing your measurables, and write your email content. We'll cover all of that in this chapter.

Create your Skills Video

Coaches cannot be everywhere to scout you. An effective skills video serves as that all-important first look. In our post-COVID world, and the limitations it created on coaches' and staffs' time and recruiting travel budgets, a skills video has become the most valuable tool in the toolbox. Student-athletes must have one. For many coaches it's the only way to see a player at all.

Every correspondence or post to a coach needs to have the most current skills video and, if possible, a good highlight video as well. If you only have the time for one, the skills video is more important. Baseball coaches are more focused on a player's skills than they are game footage. Every college questionnaire requests them. Remember, a college staff does not care about fancy editing or music. Keep your video from 2 minutes to 2 minutes and 45 seconds in length. Do not go over 3 minutes.

Because skills videos don't require specific locations or expensive equipment, they can be shot relatively easily on your own with a cellphone. I've had enormous success with VideoShow, which is a free app. It is tech idiot–proof and allows you to create a top-flight video for free.

Follow these guidelines for your skills video:

- **Basic hitting drills**. Live BP, side and front toss throws, side and back angles with only 3-5 swings (max) at each angle. Give the coaches something to see without making a feature length film. The coaches are trying to answer the question, "Can this player help me?" and the faster you can give them the answer, the more likely you'll hear back more quickly.

- **Catchers**. Receiving and blocking, pop, and release, throws to second base, back pick and throws to third base.

- **Pitchers**. Back side view and behind catcher. Give three shots of each of your pitches from each angle, with your spin rate and velo (if you have it) in a text box below the video.

- **Infield Defensive Reps**. Film the five main defensive reps (backhand, forehand, hits to the hole, arm strength and release, footwork, and anything else you feel draws attention to your athleticism) with multiple angles (back, side, front); you must try to display your ability to seamlessly execute the mechanics of the play.

- **Outfield Defensive Drills**. Catch a fly ball to your left, right, front and back. Get a ground ball to your left, right and front. Show yourself hitting a cutoff man 2–4 times after these catches and 2–4 throwing all the way to the bag (at least once to third and at least once to home).

- **Speed**. If your 60 time is below 7.0 seconds, this will be a strength; run one or two for the camera. Also, if you have good speed, show yourself hitting the ball and breaking out of the box, running all the way through the bag at first base.

Get your Skills Video Out There

Once athletes have created their video, what is next? Every coach is different, and there is no one way to get it right. Keep in mind you cannot please everyone, and you will make mistakes.

Err on the side of being aggressive getting your videos out there. I am not a fan of tagging every coach on the planet in social media posts. If you would like to select a few coaches with whom you may already have had contact, it is fine. However, it is more important in the post to have your social contact info, any of the ways the coach might get a hold of you, and your 60 time, velocity, spin-rate, GPA, SAT, etc.

Many coaches and recruiting coordinators are using The Baseball Bluebook app, Twitter, Instagram, and YouTube a lot. Coaches will use recruiting sites and programs like Perfect Game, Prep Baseball Report, or Best in US when they want to see profiles and more extensive info on a player. However, they must have a membership to those sites, and a lot of schools do not want to pay for them.

PRO TIP: Coaches are now asking for you to pin your latest or best video to your profiles on Twitter or Instagram along with all your contact info, important stats, and GPA. If they follow a video link and like it, they will be more curious to look more into you.

Sign Up with Recruiting Services

This is the time to talk about recruiting services. Just two examples are NCSA (Next College Student Athlete) and Baseball Factory. When talking about these types of services, I am speaking from a parent perspective and our budgeting issues.

Every service has pros and cons, and different levels of membership for parents to use and coaches to be able to access. I have found them to be a great organizational tool and monitoring device. Think of them as a big mall or giant outlet location. Each player sets up his profile pages and links to his measurables and videos. Every email he or she sends from that service site will automatically attach a link to their profile page. You can update your profile and videos as often as you like. Plus, you can use the service to find coaches' contact information.

Coaches, in turn, can reply to the athlete or send camp invites. They can also use the service to search for players by position, skill sets, speed, and more. They can then view their profiles and contact players directly if they like what they see. The nicest feature from a player perspective is you get notifications and can track when and if the coaches open your emails, view your profile, and or look for players in your position or with your measurables. They also post regularly about what positions and in what year they need. Upper-level memberships promise more personal interaction between their agents and the coaching staff. I am not sure that is worth the extra money it takes.

Contacting a Coach

Once your toolbox is set, start reaching out to those coaches at schools you are interested in. High school baseball players can contact a coach at any time. However, remember there are rules around when coaches can respond.

While you as a family may be tempted to send a generic email blast to several coaches at several schools, don't. Send personalized emails to the schools in which you are interested. Just as athletes want more personalized emails from a coach, coaches appreciate personalized emails from the athlete.

Be sure to properly introduce yourself, including the correct spelling of the coach's first and last name. Double check coaches' names, school names, and any personalized content that you may have copied and pasted from other emails. Don't say you want to be a Tiger when you are talking to the Ragin' Cajuns!

Be sure that you, the student-athlete, is the one writing the emails and contacting the coaches. We can always tell when Dad or Mom is writing or posting. We want to hear from you in your own voice. The email doesn't have to be long. In fact, most coaches like them short and to the point. But they should be in your own voice. The first email, text, or call is always the hardest, but it gets easier.

PRO TIP: Practice! Practice making those calls. Write rough drafts of emails and texts. And always follow up an email with a phone call. Leave voice messages.

Besides including why you're interested in their program (and why you think you'd make a great addition to the team) make sure the coach has:

- Your general information, like your name, contact info, and graduation year
- Academic info, including GPA, test scores, and potential major(s)
- Your highlights video and simple measurable from a verified resource (e.g., 60 yd dash 6.8 at X Showcase)

Use the following lines to write notes about what you'd put in your email.

_____

_____

_____

_____

_____

Finally, keep the subject line clear. Here's a format to follow when emailing a coach: name, GPA, 60-yard run time (only if you are a position player and it is below 7.0), other measurables (height/weight, fastball velocity if you're a pitcher) that would separate you from your peers, contact info, the word UNCOMMITTED, and your graduation year.

A subject line would look like this: Eddie Smith // 3.44 GPA // 1260 SAT // Class of 2024 // 82 mph FB // RHP & SS // Video Attached // UNCOMMITTED.

PRO TIP: Double-check whom you are addressing the email to. If Coach Johnson is at Western State and Coach Smith is at State University, make sure Coach Johnson doesn't get Coach Smith's email or video. And don't forget to attach the video! Yes, I've done it and have received such emails; it happens.

Do Your Homework: Spend Your Money & Your Parents' Money Wisely

From the very beginning of the recruiting process, families should be sitting down together to discuss what kind of budget they will have (or not have) for events, tournaments, and camps. Unfortunately, not every family has the same budget to spend. Not every one of these events is the same, either. The following are the three options that I believe provide the best overall value. This is a list gathered after 30 years of experiencing the circuit from every level—player, coach, and parent. If you do your homework and use guides like this, you can make it happen.

College Camps

These are fantastic and tend to be a more easily affordable option for student-athletes and their families. Depending on the college or university running the camps, the number of days (usually two), and the number of other schools' coaches attending, the cost is usually under $200. Some may be a bit higher if they are longer than two days. Lodging is not included. Multi-position or two-way (pitcher plus position) players can cost a bit more.

Be aware that by NCAA rules, a Division 1 school cannot have other Division 1 school coaches attend their camps. However, it is common for a Division 1 camp to have coaches from several Division 2 and 3 schools in the region at their camps to help run them.

College camps are a great way to be seen, get valid measurables, and to be evaluated in a more personal setting by the coaches themselves. A couple benefits of a camp are a visit around the campus (usually a tour is included) and experience playing on and in the facilities. I always recommend using camps to unofficially visit the schools that you have a sincere interest in, and that hopefully have shown an interest in you.

It's important to know that once you attend your first big tournament or showcase camp (details on those are up next), the emails with camp information will come fast and furious. Many camps are the primary way a baseball program funds their budget and pays their volunteer coaches. That does not make camps a terrible thing.

However, do not assume that because you receive a camp invite it means the staff is interested in you the player. Oftentimes, they are interested in your entry fee. Look closely at the email. If it mentions seeing you at a particular event, and you remember that event, that is a good thing. It does not hurt to email that coach back personally to let them know you will or will not be attending that camp. If the email does not say something to that effect, it is a bulk mailer. You can still email or text that coach back and ask where they may have seen you play. This does not mean you should not attend camps you hear about through a bulk mailer, but be selective in your choices—especially if budgetary considerations are critical.

When you are budgeting for camps and any other recruiting tournaments or events, you always want to be sure it is a school that you have interest in and a realistic chance of attending, both academically and athletically. Do your research, reach out and ask questions, and always attach your skills video. Make smart choices.

Showcase (Team) Tournaments

These tournaments are already in your travel teams' budget. Many times they are five to seven days long and hugely attended by college head coaches and their recruiting coordinators. In the weeks and months leading up to those events, every tournament gets a commitment letter from all the program decision makers who will be attending, at every level. They then use that list to promote the event. You should be looking to see if the programs you are interested in or have created a dialogue with are attending. If they are, the next step is to text or email those coaches to let them know you will be there. Send them your game schedule for the week when you get it. The most expensive part of these events is the costs of the stay.

PRO TIP: Look for an Airbnb or VRBO. Try to share a house with other team families with a kitchen, etc., or share a large hotel room with another team parent. Go food shopping! Plan and make your breakfasts and lunches. Budget to pay for dinners out a few times.

Showcase Camps

Showcase camps are run by recruiting companies or services. Approximate costs can vary greatly; prices for a small camp with a few smaller Division 3, NAIA, and JUCO schools might be under $200. However, others can run more than $1000. They are usually a two-day event. Day 1 is frequently focused on gathering measurables (60 time, infield/outfield velocity, 5 ground balls or 5 fly balls, batting practice rounds), with some instruction. Day 2 is usually game day. Athletes are randomly put on teams, with rosters of 25 or more and lots of pitcher-only players.

The bigger the camp is, the larger the rosters will be. There are nine-inning games with rules in place to display the pitchers and incentivize the hitters to swing the bats. The first time your athlete attends one of these events is the most challenging. As a hitter it takes some getting used to. Showcase camps are not all the same—some are definitely better run than others. Some Day 2 experiences are better than others; some are much better. We all know the names of the biggies, and I will not go into listing them or reviewing them here. I will say, however, do not assume that if they cost the most or say they have the most coaches that they are the right camps for you. An example of a potentially wonderful camp with fewer coaches would be a showcase camp for highly academic schools. If your transcript matches such schools, these can be wonderful places to find your match.

PRO TIP 1: You can ask to play in the morning games. Coaches are more likely to be focused, and it is usually cooler. Stay away from the ones that only have two games for the day scheduled on say one or two sites; rosters balloon to 30 or more. The best set up is usually a Day 2 on one site with three games scheduled. ALL eyes are on one field, games run at a faster pace, and hitters see more at bats. If not, rosters are too large. You will be lucky to see two or three at bats.

PRO TIP 2: Athletes, once you are on the field, look for your opportunities to stand out, your opportunities to *flash*! If you're fast, steal every bag you can! Be the first one on and off the field. Use any chance you must show your speed. If you are a power guy, go for it! If you really know what you are doing in the outfield, dive for the ball whenever you can. Play every position they will let you. Run everything out. Hustle on and off the field. Shake hands, make eye contact, talk to the guys in the dugout with you, and cheer them on too. Talk to the coaches, pick up the trash, and thank them when your day is done.

Official Visits

During the recruiting process, a college coach may invite you to pay a visit to campus. There you will be able to evaluate the college and see if it is a right fit for you. The *official* label means the school will be paying for all or part of your trip. At each division there are restrictions to taking official visits.

- NCAA Division 1 schools allow taking official visits on September 1st of your junior year. You are only allowed five official visits, and a family member may accompany you on each one.
- NCAA Division 2 schools allow taking official visits starting June 15th after your junior year. You are also only allowed five official visits, including any you take to a Division 1 school.
- NCAA Division 3 can take official visits after January 1st of their junior year.
- NJCAA Division 1, 2, and 3, coaches are allowed to contact athletes whenever they want. In terms of official visits, they are allowed to pay for one official visit to campus and the athlete has to have finished their junior year of high school.
- NAIA Divisions 1, 2, and 3 do not restrict contacting a coach or visiting campus. You are able to take as many as you want and whenever you want. These are always paid for by your family.

On official visits, you will meet the coaching staff, athletic trainers, strength and conditioning coaches, players, and other faculty. You will tour athletic facilities, classes, dorms, library, cafeteria, and other campus amenities. You may also meet with a faculty member of your intended area of study where you will be given general guidelines of the coursework required for your potential major.

Unofficial Visits

Unofficial visits are visits to colleges that are completely funded by the visiting recruit and family. You can take as many unofficial visits as you would like (and can afford) to any school that you would like. Just be sure you are eligible to talk to the coach during your visit before you plan everything. A first-year student or sophomore may schedule an academic visit to an institution like any other prospective student would. However, they are not allowed to engage in conversation with the coaching staff while on campus. In your junior year you can start taking unofficial visits that are similar to the official visits described previously. Unofficial visits are being de-emphasized in today's recruiting world.

Any time you visit a school (officially or unofficially), prepare questions for the coaching staff and players regarding the baseball program, academics, and college lifestyle. Another factor to be prepared for is trying to assess the honesty of the coaching staff. You must try to determine, as clearly as possible, where they see you fitting into their program for the short-term and long-term.

Whether they offer you a full-ride scholarship or walk-on offer, do not feel pressured to commit while on campus. Take a few days to weigh your options before giving the program your decision.

Notes

_____

_____

_____

_____

_____

Parent and Player Questions for Coaches During Visits

Now we've reached the point where your college choices are narrowed down, first communication has been or will be established, and school visits are beginning to be scheduled. Let's see if we can help guide you and your parents through those first conversations with coaches. The following are samples of some questions parents can ask during coach's visits:

- We have researched the college and his academic goals can be met here, how are you prepared to help him with his athletic goals?
- With the portal now a mainstream part of college sports, how does the coaching staff view the portal and what does the program see as a successful way to use the portal?
- For the position you see my son playing, what is your depth chart not only next year but in early high school commitments that might affect him in later years?

- What is your graduation rate? How do you judge the success of your student-athletes?
- What academic support systems are in place? Do you have mandatory study halls? How do you monitor, if at all, your student-athletes in the classroom?
- What value do you put on and do you have systems in place for the mental health of your athletes?
- What value do you place on technology, statistics, and video analysis in your program?
- What kind of summer requirements do you have for the athletes, and do you help place them in college summer leagues?
- We have watched your program and have seen the culture of your players. That's why we are here. Do you see the culture changing in the future because of what is happening at many schools?
- We are not only picking the college as a four-year plan, but also picking you as a head coach and your staff. Do you foresee any changes in the near future?

Notes:

_____

_____

_____

_____

_____

What Does The NCAA "COVID" Extra Year of Eligibility Mean to You?

If you follow college sports or your student-athlete is closer to the end of high school than the beginning, then you probably know college student-athletes are given five academic years to play four seasons of their sport. That fifth year is called a redshirt year. Historically, it's been used to cover either academic progress, physical progress, or injury.

COVID changed this. To make up for pandemic's impact on college athletics, all three NCAA divisions, the NAIA, and NJCAA ruled that participating in a sport during the 2019-20 academic year does not count toward student-athletes' four seasons of competition. They called this eligibility relief. NCAA Division 3 and NJCAA took things a step further and granted eligibility relief for the 2020–21 academic year as well. Effectively, student-athletes were given up to six academic years to use up their four seasons of eligibility, because a medical redshirt season is still a possibility:

- A 2019–20 first-year student is eligible to play baseball through the 2023–24 academic year.
- A 2019–20 first-year student who then has a medical redshirt season is eligible to play baseball through the 2024–25 academic year.
- A 2020–21 first-year student at an NCAA Division 3 or NJCAA school is eligible to play baseball through the 2025–26 academic year.
- A 2020–21 first-year student at an NCAA Division 3 or NJCAA school who then has a medical redshirt year is eligible to play baseball through the 2025–26 academic year.

For all schools at all levels, rosters were also expanded to manage the additional students. The combined effect of students with additional years and teams with additional roster spots has created several years of chaos among current college student-athletes and prospective ones.

How Will This Change Baseball Coaches' Recruiting Needs?

Due to the extra year of eligibility and recent changes in the MLB draft, college coaches now see more student-athletes returning to campus for another year. Programs have more players and more experienced players available to them. To stay competitive, they'll be recruiting more from the transfer portal and JUCO ranks.

How Should 2022 Through 2024 Recruits Approach the College Recruiting Process Because of These Changes?

Recruits need to be prepared for a delayed recruiting process. As college coaches navigate this new environment, they first need to work with current roster spot holders to determine who plans to take advantage of their extra year of eligibility. Only then will they know how many roster spots will be available for the incoming class, and which positions should take priority in the pipeline. With no rules set around when student-athletes must make this decision, college coaches may have to delay their recruiting process as they wait for these decisions to be made.

What you should do in response to this is regularly and proactively reach out to college coaches. Ask if they know how many seniors plan to return and what roster availability looks like for the coming year. Keep in mind that coaches may not always be able to provide an answer. But this shows your interest in their program, while also helping you evaluate whether the program is still a realistic college option.

High school student-athletes graduating between now and 2024 also need to be honest about their options. You may need to revise the list of schools you have been targeting. This also means that some students who would have been considered recruitable in prior years may find themselves on the outside looking in. So, if you consider yourself a Power Five–quality student-athlete, you might need to investigate mid-majors, NCAA Division 2 or 3, JUCO options—or take a PG year.

Can Attending a Postgraduate/Boarding School Increase Your Chance of Competing in College?

Should your family consider a postgraduate year for your son? When considering this question, the most logical first step for most of you is to ask, What is a postgraduate school exactly? In some circles, spending a year in a postgraduate school will also be known as taking a PG year. A postgraduate year is often considered an academically focused or a physical development gap year (or both), like the thirteenth grade. Not every postgraduate school is a boarding school (some have commuter options), and each one has its own goals for their PG students. Some are honestly much more athlete focused. That is, they're focused more on developing skills and creating a path directly to professional baseball. Others have excellent academic curriculums, whose primary goal is to prepare each of their student-athletes for college, including Ivy League, Near Ivies, and the Service Academies. Neither postgraduate option is better or worse than the other. It depends entirely on what is the best match for you and your goals.

Families often focus on boarding schools, as they have established, built-in support systems. They typically have a team of experts and advisors who focus on *every part* of *everyone* in the program. The board of advisors usually will include academic teachers, college placement advisors, experienced coaches, athletic and personal development staff, plus on-campus mentors and more. Simply put, those advisors are so important and great at their jobs, you will want to take them home after that PG year to run your lives for you forever! By doing a PG year, you are growing your support system. When a student-athlete feels supported, they are more confident and better equipped for next-level success.

Independent schools that offer a PG year often stand in stark contrast to a conventional high-school experience. Often, they are prestigious and selective boarding schools with large endowments and generous, need-based, forgivable financial aid (i.e., not loans). Many of these postgraduate schools are in New England, with several in the Mid-Atlantic and increasing numbers in California and Texas. They are populated by students in grades 9 through 12, plus the postgraduates. The student body, as well as faculty, come from across the country and globe. Unless they are commuters, students live on campus in chaperoned dormitories, and are taught and coached by faculty members who also live on campus. These independent boarding schools can feel much like small colleges, with academic offerings that can accelerate beyond college advanced placement. Some of the oldest and most prestigious schools are on sprawling 500-acre campuses, with multi-million-dollar facilities for academics, athletics, and residence life.

This is often overlooked, but upon graduation, you become part of a network of alumni that tends to be loyal, far-reaching, and extremely influential. These types of alumni networks can be helpful in every field of

71

post-baseball vocational choice—from medicine to teaching/coaching to business to real estate to law and beyond.

For athletes, a true benefit of attending a postgraduate school is the luxury of being able to communicate to college coaches, "Hey, remember me? I was class of '23. Now I'm class of '24. You have another year to recruit me! And I'm spending my extra year as a postgraduate at School X. I will emerge bigger, faster, stronger, and better at my sport. My academics will be a notch or two above what they were when you last saw my transcript."

COVID has caused so many long-reaching issues. It did not skip college baseball. Every roster at every level of college baseball is bloated with athletes taking advantage of the give-back year. As a direct result of this, many amazing 2021's and 2022's are feeling the effect. A PG year, in essence, gives that year back. It reopens doors that have otherwise closed through no fault of your own, and allows students who choose that path to knock out academic prerequisites, train for your sport, and maybe even earn some additional money while working a part time job or taking an internship in your field of choice. If done right, they can open new doors to higher profile schools that were previously unavailable due to a lower academic profile.

The summer between high school graduation and the postgraduate year is also important. It's another summer to perform in front of college coaches, all while you are (hopefully) bigger, faster, stronger, more physically mature, and savvier about how college recruiting works.

Choosing a PG year should never be seen as a step back or standing still. For those who choose to pursue it and do it the right way—taking advantage of all the opportunities available—it can be the best professional decision a young person ever makes. The tier of college options you had entering the postgraduate year remain in place. On the flipside, new, often very exclusive doors open up in college recruiting as the PG year is ending. A postgraduate year is very much a win-win proposition.

MENTAL HEALTH AND HOW IT CONNECTS WITH YOUR STUDENT ATHLETE'S SUCCESS

You may have noticed in the questions in the coach section that we mentioned mental health as an issue to address with staff. This is a massively important part of the overall health and development of young student-athletes. The pressure either placed upon them or self-imposed is immense. We often forget that these are young adults not used to or even possibly ready, emotionally, socially, or mentally to handle those pressures. It can be overwhelming to devastating effect. As the recent rash of athlete suicides has shown us, it is imperative that our sports programs confront these issues head on and put systems in place to catch issues before they start. The hyper masculine culture of sports, especially men's sports, is no exception, and needs to do everything it can to get rid of the negative stigma placed on addressing mental health issues. The topic could take up another book, but for now I am including two special sections from Brian Taylor, a former Master Trainer with Tony Robbins.

The Two Biggest Enemies of Mental Performance (aka The Twins of Terror)
by Brian Taylor

You hear a noise outside your house. It's faint. You listen closer and recognize its two people talking. You listen more carefully. They're talking about breaking into your house—and stealing *your* property. What are you going to do? How far are you going to go to protect your house and your belongings? Would you double-check the door? Would you call the police?

Here's the scary thing to me. Most people leave the door to their *mind* wide open. What do I mean by this? Those two people I mentioned earlier—the ones who wanted to break into your house—have names.

Doubt and uncertainty.

You may have experienced one or both. For 30 years I have witnessed those two you-know-what's wreak havoc, not just in athletes but in entrepreneurs, business owners, and anyone who leaves their door open.

Once doubt and insecurity are nested in your brain, all sorts of things start to happen. Self-talk, once a little kitten, is now a lion roaring in your ears. Nerves that you used to brush off as little butterflies in your stomach now become a full-blown panic attack. Then things start to happen. Maybe there's a hitting slump, or routine plays become not so routine.

Getting rid of those two is much harder once they're in your head instead of out on the street.

So, what do you do if they're already inside? How do you keep those two out? Those are both good questions, and I hope if you continue to read this you'll find some answers on how to prevent and deal with them.

Number One, Stand Guard at The Door to Your Mind

I can't state this enough. No one—let me repeat, *no one*— gets access inside your head unless *you* give them access. Okay, maybe your parent does. No one else does, though. Teammates? No. Coaches? No. Your competition? Especially no!

Allow me a rant. Coaches, and some parents, can be especially problematic here. Most of the time they are completely unaware of the damage or problems they're creating when attempting to motivate—or whatever else it is they're trying to accomplish—if they don't know how to motivate. Instead of motivating they are breaking down that door. I'm going to be very blunt here. People who don't know what they are doing with regard to mental performance or mental health need to quit running around like a bull in a China shop. They can create more problems than they're solving.

Here's a story about just how quickly the door to your mind can swing open, and how quickly performance drops when it does. I used to train with a former road bike racer who would occasionally let me in on what he called his "mind shenanigans." He would routinely go up to other racers and say

74

"Are you feeling, ok? You look sick. Do you have a fever? Your face is kind of … red." (He'd always use the words "kind of" to lessen the perceived impact, and leave it up to his competition's doubt and uncertainty.)

As you would expect, the other racers immediately responded with "Are you serious? Oh, no!" Or they would run to find a mirror to double-check their complexion. I could go on and on with the examples. I won't. This guy made a career out of opening mental doors and letting doubt and uncertainty in to run amok.

Have you heard the saying the best offense is a strong defense? Nothing could be more accurate in this case. Simply being aware that doubt and uncertainty are waiting for an opportunity allows you to be better prepared. Being better prepared allows you to see those two from a mile away.

Tell yourself this and repeat it: "Stand guard at the door to *my* mind."

Number Two, Watch The Questions

We are constantly asking ourselves questions. (And others, especially if you're younger!) "What is this?" "What do I do about this?" Questions determine what you focus on and where your focus goes. They become especially important regarding negative thoughts.

Questions can cause problems when they pry open the door and let you-know-who in. "Am …" and "Is …" questions start to take on a life of their own when coupled with the right—that is, wrong!—language. "Am I good enough?" "Am I going to strike out?" "Is that pitcher throwing gas?"

"Why …" is the most problematic of all question beginnings. Think about it this way. There is no definitive answer to a "why" question. "Why did I strike out?" Well, take a seat and let your brain roll the scroll on every possible reason. "Why did I miss the ball?" Whew! You'll be here for a long time while your brain comes up with every conceivable answer. Those are like fast-track passes for doubt and uncertainty to come flying in.

Now, let me be clear, I'm not going to say you should never ask why something happened; there's a time and a place. More than likely, during or immediately after the game is not it.

Let me give you a way to illustrate how questions change our focus. You can do this with a friend or family member: "Look around the room you're in and find everything that is green. There will be a test. Make sure you find everything that is green. Do you have a good list in your mind? Now, close your eyes. Tell me everything that's brown."

Did they laugh?

Now ask that person to open their eyes and look around. Do they see the brown now? That's because the question changed their focus.

So, if you find yourself asking something like "What if I do badly today?" then ask yourself "What if I do well?" Teach yourself as early as you can to avoid questions that cause you to focus on negative things.

Please tell yourself this and repeat it: "Ask better questions if I want better performance."

Number Three, Tone and Language

While I'm not going to debate whether it's your words, tone of voice, or body language that have more of an impact on the people around you, I will take a stand on something. Your tone and language impact your mind, especially when it comes to doubt and uncertainty. There's nothing like a whiny tone to set them off. Couple a whiny tone with some negative language like "I suck," and you are opening the door. Combine poor tone and language with the wrong questions and that door will fly open like it's on a spring.

Why do I suck? Why do I always strike out? Why does this always happen to me?

If you hear anything like this, do whatever you can to get your teammate, coach, or yourself to stop—immediately. Even if that's just blowing some whistle or calling their name, get them to stop. No one ever thinks the cute baby bear is going to grow up to be a 600-pound monster of a grizzly. Tone and language are the same way.

Here's an example. The fact that I work on mental performance doesn't escape my son. I'm always using him as a guinea pig for testing some new strategy or idea. In my latest test case, just for this chapter, I purchased a digital hand strength grip tester to prove the impact of tone and language. It was worth $25, at least to me, to see if I could prove to him (and you) how critical they are.

At first, he was very excited to show off how strong he was; I hadn't told him about the second part yet. I took a look at his feats of strength and wrote the numbers down. Next, I asked him to say all the negative things he's ever said and say them with gusto. "I suck! I'll never be able to lift as much as you!" I watched as he squeezed the grip tester again. The display flashed a number that was … less. Way less.

He lost 25% of his power talking all that trash to himself. He exclaimed as he looked at the number with shock.

If you notice yourself using negative tone and language, here's a way to handle it. Stand on one leg and say it again in the same tone. The difference in posture will cause you to reflect on it immediately, and you'll close that door.

Number Four, Body Language and The Home Invaders

You could call this, Which Comes First, the Chicken or The Egg? Nothing gets talked about more in mental performance than body language.

Unfortunately, most of that goes nowhere and if anything causes athletes like you to struggle more, not less. Your body language is habitual. That's why parents and coaches notice it right away. They become familiar with your normal. They notice something different almost immediately and their brains call it out. They tell you, "Change your body language," and at first you probably don't even know how to respond to that. Whatever you are doing feels normal to you at that moment. (I'm going to add a few visual cues at the end of this chapter to help you be specific with your body language assessment.)

You need to understand what your resourceful (good) and unresourceful (bad) body language *feel* like. Do this exercise. Stand like you stand when you are totally confident, like nothing can stop you. Notice everything: head, posture, eyes, breath, centeredness. Now stand like you stand when you're unsure or unconfident. You'll notice the shift. Tell yourself what the difference was. If you can't tell, repeat it. Alternate total confidence and total lack of confidence. Eventually you'll feel it.

Number Five, What Went Well–What's Not Ready Yet

This is the debrief. It's usually a loaded topic. It's about what you do after a practice or game when mistakes made, and how to address those. This is baseball; it's going to happen. The natural inclination of coaches and parents (and thus you the player!) is to talk about all the things you did wrong, and what you can do next time to improve. This is the wrong time and wrong order.

Let's be real for a minute. You know what went wrong in a game. If you were asked after a game to write down all the things you did wrong, you'd know every single mistake you made and sometimes ones that other people didn't catch.

I have heard recommendations to wait 24 hours to discuss a game. While this break might be a good thing at least regarding emotions calming down, more than likely you're just postponing the you-suck-because speech (or the I-suck-because speech if you do this with yourself). Twenty-four hours isn't going to change that. Let's start with a different way.

Start by asking what went well (WWW). Even if you had the worst performance of your life, you did something right or something well. Prepare yourself; it's going to be weird the first time you try this. Our natural human conditioning is to start with all the mistakes—everything that didn't go well. You'll have to work on redirecting yourself. Flip the script and start with what went well. At first you'll have to work on redirecting. Your job is to ask yourself, "Okay, but what went well," until you find something that went well.

Next ask what's not ready yet (WNRY). There's purposefully a big presupposition here. If you're going to practice even a bit of growth mindset, the power of *yet* will pull you through the toughest slump or dip in performance. It presupposes you're going to work to make your skills ready. It also becomes a bit safer to talk about what's not ready yet versus talking about "wrong."

I strongly recommend you use this format. It gives you a consistent method of debriefing. There are going to be times you are emotionally charged after a game or team practice. This method gives you a way to keep emotions out of the conversation. Additionally, if you lead this debrief you are empowering yourself as the student-athlete.

Body Language

How you sit, stand, and conduct yourself physically is your body language. You send messages you may not be aware of. Here are some common things to look out for with body language.

- **Fidgeting**—When you fidget, you seem nervous and uncomfortable. Shaking your foot and tapping your fingers are also distracting to others. Have smooth, slow, infrequent movements.

- **Looking Down**—There's nothing down there of interest. You look evasive and timid when you lower your head. Keep your head high and others will give you more respect. You'll feel better about yourself, too.

- **Nervous or Jiggling Feet**—Upon talking to someone, if your lower leg or foot is being tapped or moved around it could reveal you're nervous, anxious, or even impatient.

- **Standing or Sitting with Your Arms Crossed**—When you sit with crossed arms, you're covering up your heart and your midsection. This posture sends the message that you're closed and you're not going to reveal anything about yourself. Also, sitting with crossed arms portrays you're on your guard or perhaps not all that interested in what is being expressed to you. And finally, it sends a message to your brain (or body) that you are not confident.

- **Drooping Shoulders**—Drooping shoulders show you're tired or maybe even a bit bored with what is being communicated. Saggy shoulders can also signify that you're feeling unsure of your abilities.

- **Hands on Hips**—Normally, when you stand with your hands on your hips it means you're tired of waiting for something (or someone) or feel impatient.

- **Unbalanced Posture or Leaning on One Leg**—Putting too much weight on one leg sends a message to our subconscious of feeling uncertain or insecure.

Here are ways to adjust or improve your body language:

Model The Best

Watch your favorite player. How do they walk out to hit? How do they walk back if they didn't hit? How do they stand on the field? I like the saying, success leaves clues. Here's another tip. Rather than just watching, emulate your favorite player. Walk like they walk; stand like they stand. Do your best to copy everything they do with their body language.

Adjust Your Posture

The way you hold yourself and move around plays a big role in determining your mood and how others see you. Make it a habit to sit and stand with your back straight and your shoulders back. Distribute your weight evenly and tighten your abdominal muscles.

Make Yourself Big

Whether you're sitting or standing, don't be afraid to take up a little space. Spread your arms and legs slightly. Insecure people tend to do the opposite and attempt to appear small. Show that you're confident enough to claim the space around you without apology.

Make Eye Contact

Hold your head and your gaze up. If you find it uncomfortable to look someone in the eye, try focusing on different areas of their face for a couple of seconds at a time. The results will be about the same.

Open

Overall, think in terms of taking up whatever space is available to you. Uncross your arms and legs. Plant your feet about a foot apart. Lean toward someone while they're talking to you.

Slow Down

If you tend to move faster when you're nervous, experiment with doing the opposite. Make your gestures and speech more deliberate and relaxed.

Parents and Student Athletes, please sign this line after reading this section!

Athlete   _____

Parent   _____

LET'S HEAR FROM THE EXPERTS

Coaches want something from your student-athlete, and that's to use your student-athlete's ability to help their program win. They want to see a student-athlete develop and represent the school positively as they move forward in life, and hopefully give back to the school in donations of both time and money.

Student-athletes hope that program and staff will develop their ability and skill sets to fulfill their dreams to play at the professional level for a number of years. But what are coaches really looking for?

In this chapter you will read from actual conversations that Butch and I had with some of today's best and longest-tenured college coaches. Among other things, we asked them:

- Can you explain the role body language plays regarding recruiting as well as in student-athletes at your school?
- Can you explain how you and your staff coach athletes on the failures within baseball?
- When do you get a sense that younger players should start to worry and/or focus on college baseball?
- At what age do you like to start recruiting?
- How can parents help during the recruiting process?
- What role do academics play in the recruiting process for you and your staff?
- How important is character/makeup?

I strongly recommend having a highlighter handy so that you can quickly find answers to your questions on an ongoing basis. Questions arise at various times during the recruiting process. It's important to remember to stay updated on your individual process. Be accountable and take initiative with your process. This is a *life-altering* decision. You become the decisions you make!

Meet the Coaches

These coaches offer you quality advice based on decades of experience. I believe if you pay attention to what they are saying, it will help you as a family find the best possible fit for your student-athlete. While reading these discussions with coaches remember the true trade off: *athletic ability for academic excellence*. You're about to hear from:

- Tim Corbin, Head Coach of Vanderbilt University, winner of the College World Series in 2014 and 2019
- Jim Foster, Head Coach of Northwestern University (Coach Foster was interviewed while he was Head Coach at U.S. Military Academy West Point)
- Scott Jackson, Head Coach of Liberty University.
- Travis Jewett, Recruiting Coordinator for University of Southern California (Coach Jewett was interviewed while he was Head Coach at Tulane University)
- Jay Johnson, Head Coach of Louisiana State University
- John Savage, Head Coach of UCLA, winner of the College World Series in 2013
- Jim Schlossnagle, Head Coach of Texas A&M University
- Jeff Willis, Head Coach of LSU Eunice, winner of college world series 2006, 2008, 2010, 2012, 2015, 2018, 2021

Remember, get out that highlighter!

What role do academics play in the recruiting process for you and your staff?

Jim Foster, Northwestern University (questions answered while at West Point). "It's a requirement that we must meet so the question must be asked to every recruit. I constantly ask for a 24 ACT across the board or a 1200 SAT. I always ask for the highest-level math course they have taken and what their GPA is. If a player is fringy on the ACT/SAT score I will continue to recruit them if they have been successful in high level math courses and have the work ethic, drive in the classroom.

"All in all, it plays a big role—we want to find players that will be up to the academic challenges at West Point as that plays a big part in their overall success in other areas. If they can handle the academics, they will be able to properly focus on their baseball development. If they struggle in that area, it will leak over into baseball."

Jeff Willis, LSU Eunice. "Academics play a huge role when we go recruit; we want to get student-athletes that understand that their education is number one. There is a reason why it is student-athlete and not athlete-student. We want athletes that understand the classroom is a competition just like the game is a competition. We also must realize individuals are given different gifts, and the classroom comes easier to some than others. We certainly do not want to pass on those individuals if they have the want and desire to get it done in the classroom. It really comes down to a person's attitude and work ethic on and off the field."

What role does body language play in recruiting as well as in student-athletes at your school?

Jim Foster, Northwestern University (questions answered while at West Point). "Body language and mentality are big indicators of a person's toughness. Toughness is what wins our team championships. Our goal is to continue to find better players that have this toughness makeup. The way they communicate, their body language, mentality, and how they react to different situations all speaks to their ability to be able to handle a place as rigorous as West Point and speaks to their character. Our job in recruiting is to find the most talented players that will pick themselves up after they get knocked down because they will 100% get knocked down in baseball, academics, and all other areas of West Point."

Jeff Willis, LSU Eunice. "Body language is one of the biggest areas we will look at in an individual. It screams, I am disciplined, or I am undisciplined. All coaches talk about controlling the controllable. If you cannot do the simplest thing as having good body language, how are you going to respond when the pressure is on? The negative body language only supplies confidence to your opponent. It shows that you are rattled and not in control. Cool, calm, and collected!"

How do you and your staff coach athletes on the failures within baseball?

Jim Foster, Northwestern University (questions answered while at West Point). "As a team we put ourselves in as many of those failure situations as possible so that our players learn how to handle them. We make practices game-like, we practice with high energy, we prepare, prepare, prepare.

"We give the time, tools, and resources to know how to avoid and overcome failures. On the team level our preparation and attention to detail is what helps our players overcome failure. On an individual player level, we have one on one meetings, we are honest with our players, and give them the tools and resources to overcome their failures.

"We push our players to own their development, this certainly helps players push through their failures. We help our players develop in game, pre-game, and post-game routines so that they can be consistent with what they are trying to achieve. We give them information and teach them about nutrition, sleep, recovery, the weight room, etc. We give them outside resources like Captain McKague in the Center for Enhanced Performance (CEP), the nutritionist on post, yoga, etc."

Jeff Willis, LSU Eunice. "Failure is the master teacher, as you can either respond to it or run from it. How you respond says a lot about your want, desire, and character."

At what age do you like to start recruiting?

Tim Corbin, Vanderbilt University. "I think later in their high school career. Now I'm going to say some of these things, but Walter, Vanderbilt has certainly recruited younger kids before, and I think it happens all over. I don't really think that young males are in a position mentally, physically, and emotionally to make decisions of that nature until they're into their high school years, more like 10th and 11th grade and sometimes senior year. We've had a lot of good players here that have committed to us during their senior year, Carson Fulmer being one of them.

Scott Jackson, Liberty University. "First, let's be honest, all kids develop differently. They develop at various stages of life. I've got a 15-year-old and he's undersized and he's weak. Okay, I'll throw out Colin Moran of the Cincinnati Reds, for example. Colin Moran came to us at the University of North Carolina. He came to our camp when he was a sophomore in high school, and he might have been 180 pounds. It was a slow twitch look, meaning none of his skills jumped out at our coaching staff. It was a look that you thought, man, this guy's got a way to go.

"Let's fast forward two years to his senior year of high school. He still hasn't decided. Ok, I want everybody to hear this. He hasn't decided and he is in the summer before his senior year of high school and he's working out at the Northeast Classic up there. Where was that Walt? He was in the same class, I think, as Tyler was. It was at Bentley University. So up steps Colin Moran and the ball starts coming off his bat a little bit. This is in August, and next thing he's playing in Jupiter, in late October. I just kept in touch with the family, and I kept watching him and following him in Jupiter.

"Colin Moran, a future MLB player, committed to the University of North Carolina in the fall of his senior year after Jupiter; that young man did not develop until later. He didn't start to get strength until later, and he signed as a six pick in the draft in 2013 for $3.6 million. There's so much of this that I think it's hard. It's so hard to be patient with velocity. It's so hard to be patient with strength. Those blessings are going to come given time and arduous work. The thing that I want to encourage everybody to do is to just be patient with the process. It's an overused word, the process. But if you don't have a passion for just continuing to get better and blocking out the noise of what other people think and what the dugout talk is. 'Billy's committed, and Johnny's committed, and Bobby's got visits and I don't.'

"It's so easy to get sucked into that. Student-athletes think, I've gotta rush to make a decision or I'm getting left behind. This game has guys in the big leagues like Jose Altuvé and Pedro Martinez that are undersized, but they've got things that other guys don't. So, when you start looking at all this and how it plays out, I think that the end of the conversation needs to be how bad do you want to play? How much grit do you have and how much do you want to work for it?

"I'll flip back to the comparison thing. If you want to compare yourself to other people, if you want to compare yourself to players on your team or want to compare yourself to the guys that are around you that are making commitments to schools, you're going down a road that's a trap. It doesn't mean you're going to end up being Colin Moran, but it certainly does end up meaning that you're going to continue to fight through things. We've made a living at Liberty in the last three years of signing kids later rather than sooner, because those kids have had to fight to get to where they are, and they've got this edge to them that it's going to carry you and separate you when you get to a campus."

Jim Schlossnagle, Texas A&M University. "In a perfect world, I would prefer that the process not begin until the summer prior to their senior year because I think that's the best option for both parties. That's the best opportunity for a coach and a college staff to look at a player and be able to more accurately project what they're going to be when they come to college.

"That's the perfect world. That's also a time where a young man and a family are thinking about college and they're more academically and athletically mature. They have an academic transcript. They have an athletic history. They know more about what they want. Do they want a small school, a big school? Do they want to be far from home? Do they want to be close to home? What are they looking to major in?

"So that would be in a perfect world, and that's the way it used to be. Unfortunately, today, all that process is sped up, and now we are asked to speed the process up because of the rules and the level of competitiveness in a conference like the SEC; everybody is sped up. So now we're looking at players as early as their freshman year of high school. I'm not going to tell you that's a good thing, but it is what it is. My advice to a family is to try and as best you can and do as much research as you can. What are you looking for regarding a college degree? What's super important to you? And once you define that, there's no need to decide until you find it.

"If I was a family today, I wouldn't panic if I looked on social media and saw that their friends are making decisions in their freshman, sophomore, junior year. If your son hasn't had that opportunity or they haven't found the right place yet, I would not panic because talent always wins, talent plays. There's always room for a talented player. I would just be very definitive on what I'm looking for. Until I found it, I wouldn't decide until that point. Once I do find it, I don't think there's anything wrong with pulling the trigger.

Again, I do wish it could go back to the way it used to be, that a student-athletes' decision wasn't made until the summer or fall prior to their senior year."

John McCormack, Florida Atlantic University. "Walter, at Florida Atlantic we have not engaged in that early recruiting. Young people need an opportunity to develop both academically, emotionally, and baseball-wise. They need a chance to form their own opinions. They need a chance to let their careers play out, and then for us to recruit them, we must make sure there's a path to some sort of success. I know it's getting younger and younger, and we have not gotten involved in that. I don't think it's for us. It's just not productive. I'm not saying it's not productive for other people, but for us it's not.

"When I started recruiting in 1991, it was certainly much different. You didn't even really have kids on the radar until that summer going into their senior year, and you were allowed to talk to them after July 1. Then the important thing was just to get them to agree to a visit, and then you would go through the fall, they would take five visits, they would find out what they like and didn't like. Then you made offers and the guy said, yes or no. Now it is in reverse. Everybody rushes to the table to get committed just because that's what everybody's doing. Then we'll get to know each other and see if it's a fit.

"What happens with this scenario is that you might have to backtrack. Someone either says, I don't want to go there, or the school says, hey, you're not good enough. I just got a DM [direct message] from a kid that, hey, I'm opening my recruiting process again and that really disturbs me. It just disturbs me in the fact that there wasn't enough time taken to find out if that's the right place for you. Baseball is one thing, and it's an important thing, but academics matter most. Can you afford it socially and geographically?

"There are all sorts of things I don't understand as a father regarding this entire current process. I had two sons that played college baseball. I don't understand as a father how some people can commit, and they've never been there, and they've never met the coaches face to face. I'm not saying that it hasn't happened here, but we try. I want to have a conversation with them. I want to look them in the eye. I want to get to know their parents to make sure it's a fit. It might not be a fit. I think that we're putting the cart before the horse now and just to get committed. Then we'll figure out everything later. If it doesn't work, then we'll just move on and that's a major part of it.

"The young people growing up today have played on numerous travel teams. They've attended numerous high schools, not all of them, but most of them. So, for them just to move on, it's not that big a deal. Where to me, it's a huge deal for a program to become special to you. I see it a little bit differently because I've been here 32 years, and I want everybody to feel the same about FAU that I do, which I know is unrealistic."

"Okay, things are going to be rocky in the beginning for everybody, but let's let it stand the test of time. When you come to your senior year, the end of your amateur career, you're going to be so much better off for it. Athletes that are in the portal now, which has worsened their recruiting situation or made it even more of a challenge for trying to take the time as a coach to develop student-athletes. As a student-athlete, if I don't like it, I could just go somewhere else. I think it's just a bad thing for young people to kind of get in their head that it's okay to back out of something and move on. We've had it happen to us several times over the last couple of years, and it's disturbing, but we're just going to keep doing the way we do it. There are enough players out there. There are enough guys that want to be involved in what we're doing. I don't really worry about it. I don't concern myself with what other people are doing."

John Savage, UCLA. "I think baseball is a lot different than a lot of the other sports. It really has moved along at a much earlier age than, let's say, football or even basketball. So, I think it's unfortunate at the end of the day that it is that way. I just think that at the end of the day, if you're a solid player and you're getting better, you're growing. Ninety feet is a long way. Sixty feet, six inches is a long way. It takes time for everyone to really be able to handle, really, the measurements of the game, truth be told. And throwing from right field all the way to third base on a line, be able to long hop that, be able to run a good 90ft, be able to hit a ball, not only a pulled ball, but a ball opposite field driven. So, I think at the end of the day, there's so many opportunities.

"You don't want to jump on an opportunity—your first opportunity. You want to see what's out there. I think that's safe to say you don't want to rush;

you've got to believe in your abilities. You don't want to be scared into thinking that this may be my only opportunity for me to do something. Now, if it's your senior year and it's June and you have one opportunity, of course you're going to take that. But I think I really hope we can get to a point where we can move it back a little bit. Let sophomores play varsity. Even if you're a freshman, let them play varsity. Let them see how they do against older players, let them compete at that level, and then have colleges be able to get in after their sophomore year. I would absolutely sign up for that right now. It's about taking care of business. It's about making sure that you're doing well in school, that you have options.

"So, I was saying I think you just must believe in your abilities. Obviously, you want to get exposure, but at the end of the day, they're going to find you. Regardless of where you're at, they're going to find you. There are too many people out there that are scouting, that are running travel teams, and are working high school programs. Baseball is a small community in many ways, and they talk a lot among themselves. If you're a good player or you're a good pitcher, the word spreads. And so, it's about being a good teammate. It's about being a good player on your team. And then eventually, obviously, you'll get exposure and you'll be able to have options."

When do you get a sense that younger players should start to worry and/or focus on college baseball?"

Jay Johnson, Louisiana State University. "I think the first thing that's important is to be the best player on your high school team. And what I mean by that is—and I know not all high school baseball situations are created equal, that this may not sound like conventional wisdom—but I've always looked at it this way. If you're going to be a top-level player in Division 1 baseball, you kind of have to master, conquer the level that you're at first. So, I think being the best player you can be for your high school team to where the coach wants to pick up the phone, call an LSU, and say, Hey, I really got a guy that can help you win a National Championship, this guy has a chance to be a future professional player. I think getting on the same page with that high school coach and doing a solid job for him is important.

"I think what gets lost a lot of times for players is they want the end destination; they want to post on social media that they committed to a school when really most of the time your thinking *should* be about improving and developing. By doing that you're widening the ranges of opportunities and creating opportunities for yourself."

How are you able to project their skill sets for your program?

Jay Johnson, Louisiana State University. "I think to your point as to identifying student-athletes I have more of a vague answer, but I think it will paint a good picture for everybody. If we're going to move forward on a player, after identifying them, I must be able to shut my eyes and see them on the field in Omaha doing something to help us win a game. Now, position by position, that's an entirely different criterion. You're talking about being good enough to be on the field with the last eight teams out of 300 in college baseball and making a difference in making your team better than the team that you're playing."

How can parents help during the recruiting process?

Tim Corbin, Vanderbilt University. "I just think that when you think about college baseball, it's one of the first large decisions that we make as an adolescent. When you partner up with a university or a school, a parent is helping their child. They're lending their child to an institution in hopes that that supervision and the staff will be creating an environment of progressive growth academically, socially, emotionally, and athletically. It just becomes a lifetime decision. Most times its life altering in so many ways. The people inside that environment have a chance to be some of the most influential people in that person's life. I think being at such a large decision, we must ask ourselves why are we saddling a young kid with making that decision at one of the most vulnerable times of their life?

"Young males at the age of 14, 15 and 16, they act on impulse, emotions. They act before they think. They don't have reasoning skills; they don't really pause to consider their actions. I think in a lot of ways they misread social cues of adults. So, when you think about the importance of the decision and the kids making it, they're not fully equipped to make that decision, which is a lasting impact on their life. So really, who's guiding them? Who's guiding them is adults. Sometimes it could be the parents, it could be people that have an interest in that kid.

"I think you must go back and think about why we're doing what we're doing and when we're making that decision to do it. Because really, it's a marriage. I think when you think about marriages, you're thinking about going through experiences in a marriage situation, dating. So, if you're a young kid looking at universities and schools, it makes a tremendous amount of sense for that young kid just to take his time and date, so to speak. Just see other places, see schools, see the fit, because it really is a fit more than anything.

"When you're a young kid and you're deciding on a school, you have no earthly idea what that situation is going to look like four or five years removed from the time that you made the decision. The reality is in making that decision, it's really about a situation that's going to create some type of calm and normalcy for you or just a place where you feel like you can grow because the people around you and the institution itself or places fit your style of personality and fit the type of person you are.

"I think in a lot of cases, Walter, we don't know that. We just don't know that until we're 16 and 17. And I think so much of what we do right now is expediting life. We're speeding things up rather than slowing these things down for young people, so they have a chance to make decisions with a sense of clarity and a sense of calm. I think a lot of probably what you're going to ask me tonight is we got to ask about our participation as adults and how we're creating these environments for our kids to help them and guide them rather than put roadblocks in their life that they must overcome because of quick decisions and quick decision making on large ticket items in our life."

Jim Schlossnagle, Texas A&M University. "I would say that the one thing that parents need to really dive in and understand is college baseball is the most underfunded scholarship sport in all of college athletics. If you think that investing $30,000 to $40,000 over the course of four or five years of summer baseball, travel baseball, lessons and all that kind of stuff is important, understand, you may be investing $40,000 to get $10,000. So sometimes saving your money is the best thing, so that when that late bloomer becomes available, you may have to pay a little bit more on the front end because the scholarship money isn't quite as available. I know this at this level in the SEC, every single coach in our conference, if a great player walks on this campus who's not committed or signed in his junior or senior year, if they think that guy can play at their school, they're going to find a way to make it happen, period.

"So, the kid who's a late bloomer, do not panic. I mean, not that I was some talented player, but I know what I looked like at 14 years, 15 years old, versus what I looked like physically at 17 and 18. So I wouldn't panic at all. Just let the process happen and it's going to work out the way it's supposed to work out, I have no doubt.

"Walter, I want to finish with this, I say this to every recruiting class. I say it to every recruit that ever steps forward on our campus. The biggest jump that you'll ever have in your career as an amateur player is between high school and college baseball. It is a massive jump from being at whatever high school you're at. I don't care how successful it is or how successful your select team is. To go from high school to any college program especially elite Division 1, SEC, SEC West caliber baseball—the next jump from college baseball to professional baseball is not nearly as big.

"I don't think there's any college coach out there that's going to walk away from a great player. There may be scholarship situations. There may be things you have to work through. It may be less affordable on the front end and more affordable on the back. There's a lot of different ways now, depending on the level of play, depending on the University. There are all kinds of ways today. So, talent and character and a kid who's a good student, that always wins."

How important is mental toughness, work ethic, and character to you in your players?

Scott Jackson, Liberty University. "I could care less if you're playing on the varsity or playing on the junior varsity. Do you have enough ability? Number one, do you have the character and the grit to fight and to get on our campus and make yourself better and the teammates around you better? If that's in play, then, yeah, we'll continue to follow you and continue to recruit you if you've got that ability level. I think there's a rush to this that, really, the older I get—it rubs me wrong.

"There doesn't need to be a rush here in a lot of cases. I think a lot of times the rush is exactly what you referred to as we started this conversation.

The rush is because of the comparison to other people. Your career is *your* career, nobody else's career. Your process is your process. There are no two recruiting processes that are identical. So, if you can just keep your feet on the ground and continue to pursue what matters. What matters is development, baseball wise. I would put the character before the development, and let's see where you end up.

"If you'll keep your head down and you'll keep fighting for what you believe in, then I think you'll find yourself in a good place. There are so many good programs out there. NCAA Division 1, not to mention Division 2, Division 3, junior college and NAIA. There are opportunities out there. Just fight to be part of them."

Jay Johnson, Louisiana State University. "If we commit to a freshman or sophomore in high school, we're not interested in the player you are today. I'm interested in the player you're going to be three to five years from now. There's a lot of days between now and then. So, we want to help them understand the necessary routines and disciplines needed to put themselves in position to be successful when they come and play for us. By doing that, it ends up usually being a better, what I would call marriage, because the expectations are clear. We help them along in that process, and they also become more prepared to be successful when you coach them. So, I just really try to communicate well, and that's helped us have success with getting freshmen on the field. You mentioned Daniel Susac, Jacob Barry, and TJ Nichols. All those guys were key parts of that team, and they were ready because we communicated the expectations to them. They did the work to be able to help get them between the lines early in their college careers, and now they all have great, great futures in front of them.

"I talk about character a lot. I mean, it's one of our three core values of our program. So, if I'm going to entrust a scholarship and entrust the result of a high leverage SEC or top 25 type game and this person, I want to be able to trust that their ability is good enough and trust that their character is good enough to train the way that they need to do both mentally and physically to create an advantage for our team."

Tim Corbin, Vanderbilt University. "I think if I had to put it [character] just in a one sentence form, I would just say 'someone who has a high care level for what they're doing.' If you think about people in general that have a high care level for everything that they do, they have a high care level for how they act, how they represent their family, what they do, how they do it, how they meet people, how they demonstrate gratitude, how they demonstrate effort. It's just a general care level for everything in their life."

How important is persistence as it relates to developing within a program and not running to the transfer portal?

Travis Jewett, Recruiting Coordinator, University of Southern California (questions answered while at Tulane University). "As a family it's important to remember, when you choose a college, you're choosing a career. It's a three, four, and in some cases, five-year decision. A lot of times in life, things don't always connect or fit right away. so, you've got to just have what we call stick to it. You've got to hang in there. You got to learn. You got to get better. You got to be coachable, you got to be challenged. You got to fail. You got to learn how to compete. All those things are super important. You know, many of these student-athletes, Walter, when they get to us, they sit next to me during the games, right. Which they're not used to sitting next to their coach during games because they're all usually pretty good players or they wouldn't be here. So, you got to learn how to not start every day or be a spot starter or a pinch runner or pinch defender, an at bat here or there. As a family, you made a quality decision based on the character of the coaches, what kind of husbands and fathers they are, the ability of someplace that you would feel good about releasing your son. So that's important so he can step out of the parent's way and learn how to do these types of things.

"We just want our kids to just keep investing, man. Just keep doing it because you never know when it's going to happen. If it happens for you earlier, then that's probably a little bit of a better transition, so to speak. But, man, we spend a ton of time teaching these kids that you are part of something now bigger than yourself. Only so many guys in a 35 and we're in 40-man rosters now. Walter, what is that? Less than a fourth of them are going to get on the field at the same time.

"So, there's going to be people on the bench. You got to learn how to excel in whatever your role is, you got to accept it, and you got to move forward. If you don't like it, you just got to keep paying your rent and got to keep fighting and competing. When your time gets called, be ready.

"A quick story. I'll tell you, I talked about the kid that's closing for us now, throwing 84 when we signed him, and he's throwing almost 95 now. Also, our right fielder is back-to-back American Athletic Conference player of the week. He's in his fourth year in our program, and this right now is the first year that he's regularly started. His freshman year, he came in, he was an infielder, had some injuries, got hit in the face with an errant ball in BP when he was taking grounders at third. He's endured a COVID season. He's been in, he's been out, and here he is now hitting leadoff for us. I think he might be hitting darn close to .500 through our first twelve games. We're playing good competition, highly ranked teams.

"The takeaway from this is that he didn't give up, Walter. He didn't quit. He didn't get the transfer portal. He understood that this is where he wanted to be, and this is the education that he wanted to get, and he would do everything he could to make his impact on this program. So those are the kind of people that we want here. And I get it. It's not easy, and I understand my role as the baseball coach, but also as a life skills coach and a little bit of a stepfather. I need to manage these guys and their personalities and stuff like that. But at the same time, they got to know we love them, but only so many guys can play, and they just got to keep fighting because it's a lot like life. As adults, we can't just jump to the greener grass or next chance all the time and you've got to dig deep and put your foot down, man. It's not everybody else's fault all the time. It's like that a lot of times you got to look in your mirror and [ask], Are you are doing what you can be doing with the decision that you made? My recommendation would be for guys to hang in there, man, as best as they can and try to make it work."

How important is it for an athlete to have a defined academic, and athletic process?

Tim Corbin, Vanderbilt University. "I think there's an organizational piece to that that you can see in a young man that really matters. I think inside of our university being a private school, it's very difficult to get into. Because the kids are part of a baseball program here, they get the ability to use their baseball skills to receive a world class education. That too is a gift. Our daughter was a recipient of that as a tennis player here. If left to get into Vanderbilt on her own, she could not have gotten into school here and that goes for most of our athletes here, most of our baseball players.

"So, to get here and be consistent, you must be equipped to some degree with organizational skills and a high care level for what you're doing. I think the kids inside this program, they demonstrate that or would have had to demonstrate it because the consistency piece of showing up every day and being ready for what you're doing, being guided by a staff, but at the same time being guided in a way in which you can create your own routines, your own habits, and by doing so, you can find some consistency within. If it was just a baseball situation where only baseball skills mattered inside of this program, it wouldn't work. There's so many other activities or components of a young person that matter for that person to be exposed to any type of success.

"And usually, it's mental organization and how they treat their situation and treat the people around them. If they can't do that very well, it would make it very difficult to be part of the program here. If you're talented enough to play at this level, I think the things that are necessary for consistency is your daily routine, your management of a 24-hour day. As a student-athlete, you make over 100 small decisions before you ever leave your dorm room every day. And those decisions are not left to chance with routines because your body and your mind go into an autopilot mode where you recreate those routines and on a sequence of actions that you follow on a regular basis. Those routines guide you and they calm you and those good routines make time, your friend. If you don't have routines, they make time your enemy. I think routines become your habits and your habits become your discipline. Your habits allow you to show up. And I think when you're a college student-athlete, it's about showing up. It's about having a lifestyle that allows you to show up to class, allows you to show up to whatever you're performing in and shows up with the ability to perform.

"I think players who carry out success inside this program in consistency are people who do small things well. We're not talking about extravagant things. I mean, you're talking about just being able to be organized the night before you wake up, be organized in the morning as you do get up and follow a line of regularities where you can leave the door and feel good about what you're going to and how you're going to be performing. I think a lot of kids, when they go to school for the first time, they're having to manage life without the guidance of adults. It's really the first time in their life where they're living but not in a home with adults. It's the first time the training wheels come off. So now you're waking up, starting your day, and you're performing based on the foundational skills that you came there with.

"If you don't have those foundational skills or haven't learned them or I think better yet, not willing to adjust to them, then it makes it very difficult to show up and get on, get inside of a classroom, and perform, get on a baseball field and feel at peace with, okay, my day started off well. I feel like I'm ready to go. I feel like I'm ready to compete inside this environment. I'm clear. I've got enough sleep. I've eaten well. It's a lot of those small decisions that you make that have everything to do with just showing up well before you even start performing. So, I think a lot of times we get caught up in how we're going to perform, but we haven't given ourselves a platform or a foundation to show up in a way that's going to enhance our abilities at the time we get in a classroom or get on the field."

SUMMARY

The recruitment process can be tricky to navigate, with all the constantly changing rules. Hopefully, we have clarified *The Process* a little better for you! Deciding what level, you want to play at in college and what school you feel your best fit takes time, and we want your process to be as smooth as possible.

It is important to understand that each family will have their own unique process. What matters most is taking the proper amount of time to do your homework. Keeping the process personal will ensure a great fit for your student-athlete. When visiting a campus, can your student-athlete see themselves living there? Always know that each morning that a student wakes up on a college campus they must have a level of comfort and feel for the community. They must be comfortable with the culture of the area and most importantly the campus that their feet are on every day. Baseball is the same sport at each school, but each campus is unique and offers your student-athlete an opportunity to grow as a current student as well as a future business leader, spouse, and parent.

The college selection process is a forty-year decision. The sport of baseball should be used as a way of trading athletic ability for academic excellence. These years at the college level often represent the final years of being a part of an organized, meaningful team. For most college athletes their playing careers end at the completion of their senior year. Then it's time to hang up the spikes. What they will treasure most, aside from their degree, will be the moments and memories of teammates, friends from campus, as well as faculty that helped them reach adulthood. Many times, the friends from college years become part of wedding parties, backyard get-togethers, alumni functions, and tailgates at future sporting events. In some cases, students meet their future spouse while attending college.

Adding all these pieces together, you begin to understand the value of slowing the decision process down and making sure you are asking the right questions for your student-athlete. While many families will think "baseball first," it is critical to understand that a student will wake up each morning away from the comfort of home. Knowing that they enjoy where their feet are every day will matter more than their success or lack thereof within the baseball program. The current landscape of college life is filled with multiple social, cultural, and in some cases political hot points, and that's a good thing. The more your student-athlete can immerse themselves in campus life and learn more about our society, the better adult they will become.

A student who is proactive and fully engaged in their own personal college selection process is going to be viewed as a leader, someone who is accountable and involved in their future. This is a student-athletes' life. This is about their role on a college team as well as building the final part of their foundation for their future as an adult. A college coach is going to look extremely favorably on those student-athletes who show strong character and attention to the details for their future, rather than having those questions or topics asked or discussed by parents. The student-athlete is the one that is being recruited and will step between the white lines of competition. If you are looking for an instant separator, be the student-athlete that takes control of your entire recruiting process.

I would like to also close with this. As a dad, looking back as my sons are now 31 and 29, I wish I had taken the time to enjoy the journey more. While it sure as heck was an exciting ride for both of my sons, I truly look back and wish I had simply enjoyed watching my sons enjoy their friends and their coaches more. The highs and lows as the parent of a student-athlete truly go by in the blink of an eye. Next you will find yourself preparing for weddings and—yelp—grandchildren!

As you read this book, your student-athlete is probably worried about things like ACT or SAT tests, homework, acne, and what's for dinner. A high school student is far different than a college student. Allow your child to enjoy and embrace their "now." Avoid trying to compare your child's process to others locally or nationally. Prepare your child for the real questions that will matter most as they begin to enter the crazy world as an adult. Allow baseball to be the vehicle that takes them from teenager to adult. Make sure the college of choice truly fits your child both in the present and for their future. Years later, statistics and results will not matter as much as relationships and moments and memories. What will matter most after their playing careers have finished is who they shared the ride with.

Here's to the future, and beyond.

RESOURCES AND TRAINING TOOLS

These tools and baseball folks are products and people I personally believe in. I am *not* in any way compensated for sharing these training tools or twitter accounts. The training tools are products that I or my sons have used and found helpful. This section is simply a way of sharing with you, the student-athletes and their families, the products and people that can aid in your personal journey within the world of youth baseball!

Training Tools

Clean Fuego. @CleanFuego. https://www.cleanfuego.com/.

CleanFuego is an essential training device for any baseball player looking to learn or polish pitches, learn to better grip and release, work out subtle changes in real-time, and so much more. It helps with spin efficiency, spin direction, pitch design, axis, and grip. Pitchers learn the proper feel and release of fastballs, curveballs, changeups, and sliders.

CleanFuego Regulation was engineered to replicate the exact dimensions of a regulation baseball ($5\frac{1}{4}$oz). A CleanFuego Overweight (8oz), which also replicates the dimensions of a baseball, was created so players could easily work it into their weighted ball training programs.

Marv Training. @MarvTraining. https://marvtraining.com/.

Marv Training's band features a patented handle that was used for several years in the rehabilitation market. The handle's design incorporates a channel design that changes the lever arm. When used properly, the handle increases muscle activation in flexor pronator mass. The flexor pronator mass is known to be highly responsible for helping protect the UCL. The design also supports multiple unique exercises for arm care. However, it was for hitting movement prep that the Marv Band first caught the attention of Big League clubs. The way the handle is built supplies a proper mechanical feel for all hitters.

The next product that Longley brought to the market was the Marv Balls. These are plyo care balls with seams on them. Longley noticed many players had developed unhealthy habits with the existing slick plyo care balls on the market, most notably the "plyo cutter." The Marv Balls feature a real leather-like texture as well as seams to make the plyo care balls as close to a real baseball as possible. You can now find these balls laying around in a bullpen in every big-league park.

Caleb Longley, Hitting and Pitching Development Coordinator University of Texas. (423) 716-0646.

Mustard. @TeamMSTRD. https://teammstrd.com/.

Mustard is the technology platform that will create and make widely accessible hyper-personalized training plans for physical and mental training from two of the most successful coaches of all time: Dr. Tom House and Jason Goldsmith. Armed with a proprietary, sensor less, automatic motion identification and analysis tool, Mustard's platform conducts complex data analysis of video captured on your mobile phone, and delivers easily understandable report cards so athletes, coaches, and parents can plan actionable steps to maximize performance.

Tom House. @tomhouse.

Tom is a world-renowned expert in the biomechanics of the throwing motion. He has over 50 years of experience in Major League Baseball as a pitcher and pitching coach, and has coached Hall of Famers in baseball, football, and golf, including Nolan Ryan, Greg Maddux, Tom Brady, Drew Brees and Phil Mickelson. He has a PhD, two master's degrees and a Bachelor of Science, and has authored or co-authored 22 books and over 20 studies for sports and medical journals.

pitchLogic. @PitchlogicS. https://pitchlogic.com/.

The Pitch Logic Apps and Balls are an unparalleled effort to bring all that computer science can offer to bear for any baseball enthusiast at any level. Every ball stands for an enormous amount of research and development, all focused on delivering critical metrics and information to players as they train and pursue proficiency. We believe in empowering all players to refine their skills and achieve their goals.

PocketPath. @PFAbaseball. https://pocketpath.com/.

Dave Coggin's "Pocket, Whip & Stick" throwing and pitching course along with the pocket path arm action trainer kit is the very first comprehensive throwing instruction program that supplies the two essential keys to making consistently strong, accurate throws and pitching success.

One, you learn the correct arm action and throwing mechanics. Two, you must perfect those mechanics by repetition—by making those correct throws repeatedly.

My unique "Pocket, Whip and Stick" throwing instruction, developed over 15 years of observing the throwing form of the most successful and longest lasting pitchers and position players with elite arm strength, zeroes in on their nearly identical arm path and mechanics, which he breaks down into three simple, easy to learn phases clearly explained and demonstrated in the included online video lesson.

Pocket Radar. @PocketRadar. https://www.pocketradar.com/.

Easy to use and rugged enough for professionals and amateurs alike, Pocket Radar is ushering in a new era in speed radar technology to transform the way in which players, coaches, fans, traffic professionals and everyday consumers understand the importance of speed and data.

The Pocket Radar product line was originally inspired by a friend who had resorted to driving down the road to a police radar sign trailer to track the speed of his little leaguer's pitching. We set out to build a professional grade speed radar that would be accessible to anyone and aimed to completely redesign the radar gun from the ground up. We knew that the core radio wave technology inside radar guns had not changed significantly in decades. We decided to begin from nothing with all new technology and shrink it down to fit in your pocket.

Offseason Training

Advanced Therapy and Performance. @atpcommunity.
https://advancedtherapyperformance.com/.

Josh is the founder and President of Advanced Therapy and Performance where he oversees the growth of his performance and therapy staff around the country, develops best practices for performance and pain (surgical and non-surgical) cases, while managing national and global growth of ATP where they current treat and train thousands of throwers a year. Josh is an innovator and thought leader in the sports performance world. Most notably, he is the creator of the 90MPH Formula. The 90MPH Formula is a simple, physics and evidence-based criteria that has helped thousands throw 90 mph (or harder). The formula also supplies checks and balances to help reduce the incidence of traumatic injury, especially UCL tears in pitchers. The ATP team is actively producing a formalized study and published with IRB approval. Josh publishes the formula for free and offers daily updates on his website, twitter, and Instagram.

Josh is a Western-minded, evidence-based, practice-driven therapist who respects many Eastern philosophies when they can drive superior pragmatic results for athletes and patients. He has spent the last 13 years actively in progressive physical therapy, acupuncture, and sport performance clinics as well as 5 years as a Division 1 Collegiate Strength Coach. His goal is to always drive the fastest results for his clients to reach their long-term goals while minimizing lost games due to injury or rehab.

http://advancedtherapyperformance.com

Instagram—advancedtherapyperformance,

Twitter—@atpcommunity

http://joshheenan.com

Twitter—@drjoshheenan

Instagram—drheenan

Champion PT and Performance. @ChampionPTP.
https://championptandperformance.com/.

Champion PT and Performance is found just outside Boston, in Waltham, MA. Champion PT and Performance was founded by Dr. Mike Reinold and

Lenny Macrina, two renowned physical therapists, strength coaches, and performance enhancement specialists who have worked with organizations such as The Boston Red Sox, The Chicago White Sox, Massachusetts General Hospital, and orthopedic surgeon Dr. James Andrews' American Sports Medicine Institute.

After years of helping professional athletes return from injury, enhance their performance, and excel at their sport, they were determined to create a similar environment for the general public. They sought to recreate the elite sports medicine model used to enhance performance by creating a hybrid model of physical therapy, sports performance training, sports science, and adult fitness training. To learn more, you can visit their websites and social media profiles:

https://championptandperformance.com

Instagram—@championptp

https://MikeReinold.com

Instagram—mikereinold

https://lennymacrina.com

Instagram—lenmacpt

For those who can't train with them in person, they also have online training options: https://championptandperformance.com/online-training/

Cressey Sports Performance. @CresseySP. http://cresseyperformance.com/.

Cressey Sports Performance is a high-performance training facility founded by athletes for athletes, and those looking to make a serious commitment to their long-term health. With locations in both Hudson, MA and Palm Beach Gardens, FL, CSP trains athletes from all 30 MLB organizations in addition to a wide array of middle school, high school, and college athletes. It's not uncommon to see Cy Young Award winners, MVPs, and perennial MLB All-Stars training alongside up-and-coming teenage players, albeit on completely individualized programs. With more than 150 CSP athletes drafted over the past decade, CSP coaches understand the key principles of long-term athletic development. A one-stop-shop for baseball athletes, CSP facilities offer pitching development, hitting instruction, physical therapy, massage therapy, and nutritional guidance.

CSP's president, Eric Cressey, serves as Director of Player Health and Performance for the New York Yankees. To learn more, you can visit their website and social media profiles:

http://cresseyperformance.com/

http://www.EliteBaseballPodcast.com

Instagram—CresseySportsPerformance

Twitter—@CresseySP

http://www.EricCressey.com

Instagram—EricCressey

Twitter—@EricCressey

CSP also offers online training: https://ericcressey.com/join-the-csp-family-from-afar-online-training-now-available.

Tracy Hayes. @mobilitychick. https://www.amplifiedmovement.com/.

Tracy Hayes, aka MobilityChick, is the founder of Amplified Movement and a Movement + Mobility Specialist. She most known for her twelve-week Baseball Mobility Series launched within the MLB community in 2020 that has garnered the attention of players and strength coaches from 24 of the 30 MLB organizations, from A-ball to All-Star. In less than 2 years since her mobility series' launch, Tracy has had one-thousand enrollments in her various mobility routines and programs within pro and non-pro baseball. Tracy has been featured on MLB.com for her work with the Orioles and for personally mentoring their Strength Coach, Liz Pardo. Tracy has been a featured guest on several podcasts.

Of the pro-clients who have taken her mobility series, players spent 15-times fewer days on the injured list (four days compared to a league average of fifty days), 87 percent of her clients spent zero days on the IL, pitchers lowered their ERA by 0.63, hitters almost doubled their HR rate (80 percent increase), 80 percent of pitchers saw an increase in velocity of 2–5 mph, 100 percent of hitters increased their overall HR rate, 69 percent of pitchers increased their K/9 rate, overall pitchers saw an 8 percent increase in K/9, 40 percent of players in AAA got called up, 25 percent of players who started above Rookie Ball made the Big Leagues, 93 percent of players were promoted at least 1 level, and players were promoted on average 1.9 levels!

Rockland Peak Performance. @RPP_Baseball. https://rocklandpeakperformance.com/.

Nunzio Signore, BA, CSCS, is a certified strength and conditioning coach, the owner and operator of RPP Baseball Training and Development in Paramus New Jersey, Director of the Pitching Lab, and serves as an Adjunct Professor at St. Thomas Aquinas College teaching "Theories and applications of Strength and Conditioning." He is a writer and lecturer who has written two books, *Pitchers Arm Care* and *Velocity-Based Training: How to Apply Science, Technology and Data to Help Maximize Performance*, as well as articles for such publications as *Inside Pitch Magazine*.

For the past 12 years, he has been one of the most in-demand strength & conditioning coaches in NY/NJ area, working with players from the Twins, Angels, Yankees, Diamondbacks, Padres, and Mariners organizations to name a few. He speaks annually at clinics like Pitch-a- Palooza, Bridge the Gap, NY Coaches Convention, Be the Best, and Inside Baseball as well as lecturing to students at universities such as Springfield College, Cortland University and Penn State.

RPP uses a full ten-camera motion capture lab, Proteus motion, HitTrax and Rapsodo. They offer both in-house and remote training.

@NunzioSignore

rpp@rocklandpeakperformance.com

Phone: (201-308-3363)

Cell: (646)533-4278

Tread Athletics. @treadathletics. https://treadathletics.com/.

Ben Brewster went from an unrecruited, six-foot-three-inch, 155-pound lefty throwing low 70s, to a walk on at University of Maryland. His underdog story led to being drafted in the 15th round by the Chicago White Sox, weighing 215lbs and throwing into the upper 90s from his sidearm slot. In 2015, he co-founded Tread Athletics, the first purely remote training company for pitching development, and one of the fastest growing baseball companies in the US.

Tread's mission statement is simple, but profound: "Tread exists to help athletes rewrite their stories." Now home to over 20 coaches, they have worked remotely with over 2,000 individual high school, college, and pro pitchers since 2015. Tread has produced 38 MLB draft picks in that time, trained dozens of MLB pitchers, and have become highly sought after by MLB organizations and Division 1 colleges to handle off-season training and analysis for their pitchers. With remote training, pitchers are assigned a coach to guide them step-by-step through a year-long program that entails throwing, pitch design & advanced analytics, biomechanical analysis, nutrition, weightlifting, mobility work, and more. Every detail is mapped out, allowing these pitchers to take the guesswork out of their development and gain a competitive edge. Ben, his partner Coan McAlpine, and their team run out of a 33,000 square foot, state-of-the-art facility in Charlotte, NC, which their remote pitchers can visit for in-person training during their respective off-seasons.

Brian Taylor. @hpmentalcoach.

Equal parts student, teacher, scientist and problem solver and likened to a mentor and life-doctor, Brian's natural leadership, compassion and desire to positively impact others coupled with 25+ years of personal development and coaching expertise as a Master Trainer with Tony Robbins, and a certified trainer for Steven R. Covey. Additionally, he has engaged in one on one strategic development sessions with such influential people as Jim Rohn and has personally trained with the likes of Deepak Chopra, Brian Tracy, Mark Victor Hansen, and John Gray, just to name a few. With depth and breadth of knowledge that isn't often seen; the energy of thirty Red Bulls, and the ability to slice through traditional coaching mumbo-jumbo like a chef's most trusted blade, he will educate, inspire and propel you. A front-of-the-room powerhouse with a genuine shirt-sleeve approach, Brian will work diligently with you as you achieve your personal best.

www.highperformancementalcoaching.com
brian@highperformancementalcoaching.com
Twitter—@hpmentalcoach
Instagram—hpmentalcoach

All Things Catching

Tyler Goodro. @goodrocatching. https://www.goodrocatching.com/

For over nine years Tyler has instructed, coached and scouted thousands of youth, high school, and collegiate baseball players. He spent over five seasons playing Minor League Baseball with the Dodgers and various Independent Minor League ball clubs. He currently serves as an Area Associate Scout for the Phillies organization covering Eastern Nebraska and Western Iowa.

Chris Snusz. @under2catching.

@under2catching on Twitter and Instagram

11y former pro catcher // East Coast Grays- showcase circuit 06-16 // 500 commits // 92 draft picks // 16 MLB players // associate scout since 2008 and recent college grad

Rick Stegbauer. @190CatcherTD. Owner/Instructor, 1.90 Catcher Training and Development.

Twitter—@190CatcherTD

Instagram—1.90 CatcherTraining

1.90Catchertraining@gmail.com

727-480-6969

Catching is the highest calling of all leadership. In no other sport are all the remaining on field players facing one individual player except for tennis. Leadership is at the forefront of the Mount Rushmore of catching, followed by receiving, blocking, and throwing.

In what we do as an instructor or any educator it is always of the highest importance to develop the person first and the player second. Find out what makes your player who they are on the field and off and make sure you take care of the person first. As a catcher you have the greatest privilege in all of sports…to lead your peers to success!

Be the leader that your teammates need!

Infield

Trent Mongero. @CoachMongero. https://coachmongero.com/

Coach Mongero is a blue-collar baseball coach who has helped thousands of student-athletes over the years in pursuit of reaching their full potential, both on and off the diamond. Trent's top priority has always been player development, otherwise known as BTM—improving a player's body, tools, and makeup.

As an educator, Coach Mongero spent 30 years as a successful high school baseball coach in North Carolina and Georgia. With 491 wins, he is ranked in the top 40 in all time wins in the state of Georgia. Coach Mongero is also the published author of "Winning Baseball" (Book 1 and 2), a nationally acclaimed book/digital video instructional series. Trent has coached over 100 student-athletes from his high school baseball programs who have furthered their playing careers at the collegiate level and fourteen at the professional level.

Gary Patchett. @gpickit25. @PatchPD.

Gary Patchett was the shortstop on San Jose State's 2000 College World Series team. He had an 11-year minor league career with the Reds and Angels. Patchett was the Southern California area scout for the Seattle Mariners for 7 years and a 2019 MiLB coach with the Mariners. He has worked with numerous first-round draft picks, MLB/MiLB players, and top high school and college draft prospects.

ABOUT THE AUTHORS

Walter Beede

With a baseball career that has
spanned over 40 years, Walter
Beede brings a diverse background
to parents and student-athletes.
His highlights as an athlete include
All New England First Team high
school player. He received a

scholarship from Arizona State University and was selected in the Round 13
of the 1981 MLB draft by the Chicago Cubs. He has been a head coach at
the high school, American Legion, National Travel Baseball and NCAA
levels. He has also worked as a Task Force member for the prestigious Team
USA program in Cary, NC.

The parent of two sons who competed and graduated at the college level,
Walter has been through the recruiting process with both of his sons, Kyle
and Tyler. Kyle played for LSU Eunice and LSU Alexandria, and Tyler played
for the National Champion Vanderbilt Commodores. Tyler holds the
distinction of being the only New England player in the 57-year history of
the MLB draft to be a two-time, first-round selection.

Drawing from his experiences as a player, evaluator, head coach, and
parent, Walter helps student-athletes and families navigate the challenges of
amateur baseball—from the playing season and the recruiting process to
athlete evaluations. Walter has helped more than 700 athletes from across the
country over the last 25 years and has developed an extensive coaching and
MLB scout network.

Butch Baccala

Butch Baccala's baseball journey started in 1980 at Petaluma High School where they were 29-2, winning the North Coast Section Championship. Highlights of his career include being named the 1980 Northern California Citizen Savings Player of the Year, helping San Francisco State University win three Conference Championships in as many years, being named Far Western Conference Pitcher of the Year in 1982, and receiving first-team District 8 honors that same year. In 1983 he was drafted in Round 13 of the MLB Draft and signed by the Philadelphia Phillies.

After injuries, Baccala retired in 1987. In the following years he was a pitching coach and recruiting coordinator in the JUCO ranks, coached in the prestigious Alaskan Summer League, and was the Head Baseball Coach in his hometown of Petaluma (1991).

In 1989 he was hired by the Seattle Mariners to a scouting supervisor's job in Nor Cal and as pitching coach of the Mariners' Northwest team, the Bellingham Mariners. In 1992 he returned to professional baseball as Northwest Supervisor for the Atlanta Braves. In his 25-year MLB scouting career he's held jobs with the Atlanta Braves, the Cincinnati Reds, and the Mariners for a second time. Baccala has worked as an area supervisor, west coast crosschecker, national crosschecker, special assignment scout, and Major League scout.

Butch has played a part in the drafting and signing of Jay Bruce, Homer Bailey, Todd Frazier, Devin Mesouraca, Zach Cozart, Mike Leake, Justin Turner, Billy Hamilton, Travis Wood, Taijuan Walker, Mike Zunino, Chris Taylor as a National Crosschecker.

Most recently, he Started Athlete911 Baseball, a youth baseball group that helps and mentors baseball players and their families on the road map of youth baseball. Baccala lives in Lincoln, CA, with his wife Kimberly Sanders Baccala. He is the father of two adults, Lauren Baccala and Avery Baccala, and stepfather to Jack and Luke Nilsson.

Made in the USA
Coppell, TX
31 October 2022

85493474R00072